KU-297-435

THE RESCUE OF
CAPITALISM
getting
ADAM SMITH
right

THE RESCUE OF CAPITALISM

getting ADAM SMITH right

Dr. James Dyce

Foreword

by

Dr. Madsen Pirie

PRESIDENT
THE ADAM SMITH INSTITUTE

Stress Publications

First published 1990
Stress Publications
47 Water Street, Lavenham, Suffolk CO10 9RN

Text Copyright © Dr. James M. Dyce 1990
Cover design Copyright © Iain M. Dyce 1990

British Library Cataloguing in Publications Data
Dyce, James M.
  The Rescue of Capitalism: getting Adam Smith right.
  1. Economics: Theories of Smith, Adam, 1723–1790.
  I. Title
  330.153

ISBN 0-9508277-5-4

All rights reserved.
No part of this publication may be reproduced, stored in a
retrieval system, or transmitted, in any form or by any means,
electronic, mechanical, photocopying, recording or otherwise,
without the prior permission in writing of Stress Publications.

Printed in Great Britain by
The Lavenham Press
Water Street, Lavenham, Suffolk CO10 9RN

DEDICATION

To Duncan Forbes M.C., M.A.,
Clare College, University of Cambridge
who introduced me to
the history of modern political thought and
the 18th century Scottish Enlightenment.

THANK YOU to my advisors and encouragers:

My academic friends: Edward Goulding M.A.
Rev. Harold Griffin M.A., L.L.M.
Prof. Max. Harrison F.R.C.S.
Francis Smith M.A.

The President, Adam Smith Institute, London: Madsen Pirie Ph.D.
The Director, Adam Smith Institute, London: Eamonn Butler Ph.D.

My publishing adviser: Leonard Brown, Production Director,
A. and C. Black.

Professional colleagues: Tom Heesom B.D.S., L.D.S.,
M.G.D.S.R.C.S.
Roy Mewton L.D.S.
Anthony Norcliffe B.D.S.(Hons)
George Richards L.D.S.
Ian Scantlebury L.D.S., B.D.S.
David Stone B.D.S., D.D.S.
Gordon Williamson B.D.S.

Fellow research workers: Wm.Jaeger M.A.
Terence and Barbara Guilbride.
Isabel Smith

Kirkcaldy District Council, Public Relations Officer: John Ramsay
Kirkcaldy Museum and Art Gallery, Curator: Andrea Kerr
Practical support which was indispensable:
Christine Pieroni
John Gwilt.
R.L.Day and Keith Willers
Patrick Colquhoun.
Angela Casey.
Heather Hopcraft Fripp

My Editorial Board: My wife.

CONTENTS

FOREWORD

By Dr Madsen Pirie, President,
The ADAM SMITH INSTITUTE

Dr Dyce takes us back and forward between the Eighteenth Century world in which Adam Smith lived and wrote, and our own complex world of an extended international order.

His highly personal insights into Adam Smith's thinking reveal lessons which Smith's discoveries hold for us today.

Dr Dyce draws upon his own expertise in relation to medicine, dentistry and the study of stress, to bring out the value of Smith's insight.

I enjoyed his book.

A Note to the reader

This work pays particular attention to Adam Smith's book, *The Theory of Moral Sentiments*.
It is important to note the difference in meaning of the word *sentiment* in Smith's early use of it, and today's meaning.

Sentiment
The Shorter Oxford English Dictionary

revised by G. W. S. Friedrichsen
Third Edition,
Oxford University Press 1973
quotes its meaning in 1639 as what one feels with regard to something; mental attitude (of approval or disapproval, etc); an opinion or view of what is right or agreeable.
For Smith it was the investigation of mental attitudes in human nature. Today the word implies emotion, not reason.

The Oxford English Dictionary

prepared by J. A. Simpson and E. S. C. Weiner
Second Edition. Vol XIV
Clarendon Press, Oxford 1989
6a   1708 SWIFT Abol.Chr.Misc. (1711) 154, I shall handle it . . . with the utmost Deference to that great and profound Majority which is of another Sentiment.
6b   In wider sense: An opinion, view (e.g. on a question of fact or scientific truth) ? obsolete.
9   In general use. Now chiefly in derisive use, conveying an imputation of either insincerity or mawkishness.

Throughout these essays, some of the spelling is repeated in the Smithian style, with a capital letter at the beginning of a word.
Those turned into anchor words for this Smithian searcher.

PART I
THE 25-HOUR-DAY MAN

If you have not heard of Adam Smith, then you are a modern, and may have missed the way.

This is my view, having practised at the sharp end of my profession in Harley Street for a life-time, having attained the usual success labels such as the writing of books and 'the world lecture circuit' in my speciality.

I knew *NOT* the father of Capitalism.

If you have a political view for yourself which ends in ISM, you are a modern, and may have missed the way.

This series of essays has the title of the rescue of an ISM, just to sell the book. That's the modern sales system. But its target is to encourage people like you and me to research the route to the next plateau for the human race, beyond our multi-cultures.

It is much more exciting there.

Adam Smith was a real man, who beat most of us by starting the 25-hour-day at the age of fourteen. What is more, he began the deep investigation of today's requirement for success by the age of seventeen.

His strategy would appear to have been missed, but it is now available. The assumption of modern economics was just about one third of his mind.

Smith laid the foundations for the discovery that there is a parallel to the chemical D.N.A. for everyone – the fingerprint for every personality.

Following this up today produces three effects at least – the real answer to stress – the reconciliation of today's conflicting antinomies – an opening to the next plateau for civilisation.

Adam Smith had a grand design.

Chapter 1

WHY WRITE ABOUT ADAM SMITH?

Adam Smith was out front in his day. He did the thinking that needed to be done at that time of global change from medieval life to industrial life.

TODAY it is not our skills which are in question, it is our thinking. We must move beyond our absorption in yesterday's world. We need to investigate the catalyst of our ideas and not flinch from the analysis. It is not, however, just an intellectual exercise.

These essays have been written for men and women like myself who have a sense of fulfilment in our calling in this world, but who have come to see that however skilled we are, the smallness of today's world compels us to open our minds to wholly different dimensions.This is not a popular position with the specialist channels of our various disciplines.

Our professional press and postgraduate programmes find it hard to accept a change of reporting, beyond the finer skills and rewards on the job. It is always someone else's task to think of the pattern unfolding in world affairs.

It is quite clear that one requires a massive filter in front of the mind when reading the national daily press. Its aim is to make money. Broadcasters also, are repeatedly challenged for their left-wing bias. The monitoring of their press advertising for new staff appears to indicate that they are not even concerned to be seen to be impartial.[1] So we look out at a scene which needs to be understood.

Why is there success in professional life yet confusion in the world?

Why the so-called stress of life when there are blockages to remove, to harness the enhancing power within our initiative?

Why not some wholly new truth?

"If an entrepreneur has not made his first million by the time he is 30, his commitment to capital growth is suspect."[2] At the age of 30 I had gone to war. At 24 my feet were on the ground as a junior associate in a prestigious private practice in Harley Street, London, and my clinical research was going very well. I was invited to launch a new department at Guy's Hospital, but a year or two later my whole future had suddenly to be examined because the nation was going to war. I'd have to give up my planned career.

Oh well, if a world war had to be, I must do something exciting and fly a fighter plane. Initiative got me past the waiting list of volunteers, I passed my Medical Board and I was into the R.A.F. Somehow or other, the more I told of my success to my friends, the thinner the story got and I had to accept that the conviction I had had for research had to be propelled at greater speed for the war effort. This could not happen as a fighter pilot. The following years unfolded an exciting tale.

Yes, by the age of 30 I had prepared to go on to the battlefield of World War II to film the methods of life-saving treatment of battle casualties where half the face might have been blown away. And no use trying to produce such a training film at a base hospital in Britain, the casualty had already got there or never would. The film included a series of eighty research stills photographs (in close sequence) taken at exposure times of one millionth of a second (1,000,000th sec.) of the flight of a bullet through bone etc., to display the full effect.

To go into battle without a gun would not receive the universal approval of the gunners, but then, what I was teaching could happen to them.... So, conviction was necessary. I had a crew of two camera men. One of them got an Oscar for one of his films after the war, so I used to tease him that it was the training he got when the dive-bombers were overhead and the flame-throwing tanks just in front of us, which had sharpened his creativeness for his Oscar winning film: *Room At The Top*. These battle films became basic training for medical and dental officers.

Today, 30 is a time for adding some questions to the ones which absorb our attention, for there is a different kind of war on today. 30 years of age is prime time, with deep conviction pushed about by the contraflows of life, and by-passes for faster heavier traffic. So how to stick to deeply held conviction and filter off the surge of propaganda?

Who is out front looking for the route over the mountains to the next plateau for mankind? No, it is not a question you can leave until you have made the next million or two. It is not the information technology chaps. They are storing memories, that's all. Yes, they speed up the options. The choices are not theirs.

Who is out front looking beyond the derailments in body chemistry? Not the cell biologists, immunologists, molecular biochemists, geneticists. What do you do with a healthy person these days?

Who is out front beyond the 'dawn raiders of the Stock Exchange' whose first concern is the balance sheet and not the lives of working folk? Not the economists, who say they believe that man's initiative means more for everyone. As it is played today, it is not so.

Who is out front beyond the complex international committees which look at the 24 wars going on in the world and do not seem to do better than fly in some food for the starving, if it reaches them? Not today's statesmen, nor the men who call themselves freedom-fighters/terrorists today and appear at the United Nations tomorrow to smile for the cameras, as gentle men.

We are deluged daily by people claiming they know all the answers or have a host of ways of saying all the trouble begins with someone else. With the opening of new channels of communication and every single authoritative voice declaring it is right, it is a pity that the cacophony should drown our ears and leave us deafened and uncertain.

It is this antinomy which needs to be addressed. Antinomy is one of today's key words.[3] The dictionary says: "It is a contradiction between conclusions which seem logical, reasonable or necessary." And that is as far as initiative today is taking us. We are obliged to look beyond this mix of excellent, valid, personal past experience.

From the beginning of time there have been periods of total disarray and then anchor ideas have penetrated the situation. The Old Testament illustrates this fact; in the same way the chemistry of a grand design in the universe has unfolded. Periods of two or three hundred years are normal when we stand back far enough to observe the designs for the human race.

We are at a period in history similar to the time when the Atlantic Ocean poured over the barriers at Gibraltar and produced the Mediterranean Sea. It was a massive movement of the earth's design. A vast change of temperature, an Ice Age receding. Little birds like house martins had to learn to fly longer and longer distances in their spring migration of thousands and thousands of miles. The Mediterranean became very wide.

How to put the needs of civilisation into the human mind? Unless they can be focused there, then there is little chance of lifting our targets to be worthwhile. The reason why they are not readily definable is because the human mind has developed electric responses which have turned into laid down pathways which are the hard facts for measuring life. There are only fleeting 'earthquake' moments in the mind when it turns to global thinking.

There is something missing from capitalism. The target of personal reward suggests that cash is the ultimate accolade for this civilisation; hardly the full dimension for explorers. The successful must know that massive national debt and today's stream of banks and companies ready to loan you any sum you care to name (and pay back almost when you wish), plus the sheer success of physical science, do not touch the questions awaiting an answer. Surges like the 'European movement' or Common Market are motored by the power of the world market. They are not aimed at answering the needs of the world. They can only perpetuate the ambitions of the leadership. There is a blockage in today's entrepreneurial mind.

Some wholly new adventures need to be set up. Something which confirms that we have a role in the course of history; so the risk is worth it. It might be remembered that Paul of the New Testament was a tent maker. It was not his tent-making which shifted the course of history.

There is refreshing wisdom from one of the Scottish Enlightenment thinkers of two hundred years ago: "It was Greece divided into many little States and 'agitated beyond any spot on the globe by domestic contention and foreign wars' that became the seat of the arts." Ferguson argued that "the Greeks achieved greatness in every walk of life *because* the laws of war were so barbarous, because they risked everything, because the stakes played for were so high and life so dangerous. (Principles II,505-7:Forbes).[4] Incidentally, the 'little States' never united and Greece disappeared as a world force.

Today, four signals should be enough warning:

1. *The Great Depression of 1990* by Dr Ravi Batra [5] gives a three sentence assessment of the world situation today: "Not only is another 1930s-style tragedy possible, it is inevitable."
"Any talk of depression today invites disbelief." "Man indeed is the architect of his own fate."

2. The last sentence in the book *Cogs in the Soviet Wheel* by Mikhail Heller [6] reads:
"On the threshold of the third millenium, the fate of mankind depends on an answer to the question: is it possible to transform human nature?"

3. The last sentence in the book *A Brief History of Time* by Stephen Hawking [7] reads:
"...for then we would know the mind of God."

4. *The Strategy of St.Paul* by Paul Campbell and Peter D. Howard [8] puts it quite clearly:
"To try to create a new structure with the same quality of bricks which failed the old, is not progress. It is wishful thinking."

What we see in the world of economics and capitalism is but the hyped-up version of the combination of information technology and the spirit of adventure. We see the flood gates open to changing ideology without a study of the forces behind the scenes and the fruit of economic handicaps which followed World War II when, for example, countries like Germany and Japan did not have to spend billions on nuclear deterrents and advanced in capitalism and headed the race.

Today we have the wisest scientific research men saying: "The century seems to be slipping through our fingers here at the end with almost all promises unfulfilled." [9]

So, what is today's target?

Nothing short of the uncovering of what to most of us is wholly new truth, right down beyond the pathology of the human mind, the paranoid condition which we attribute to human nature. We need to uncover a genetic fingerprint of nature for each one of us, as unique as the now proven chemical gene design for every single person. Within this lies the key to the future of civilisation.

The chemical genetic fingerprint, which proves that you are you and no one else, has global ramifications in its future application. More than that, it supports the essential belief that the Author of Nature has a precise plan of global dimension. Any spring-time glen of daffodils is full of perfect specimens.

How about our human nature? We have developed a complex nature which has emerged from our heritage. And what a complex of heritages there is in the world. The scientists went far enough with cell engineering to uncover the precise DNA structure. If people are as unique as is now proven, it is time we considered a parallel structure for our nature, our personality.

Just suppose this pattern is hidden because of what we call human nature. If we knew the formula, then Mikhail Heller's hope is practical and human nature can be understood and can change. We could off-load the handicaps to a perfect genetic fingerprint for each of us. A new pattern of civilisation is thus made available. It would be just as world shaking as the news of the dropping of the first atom bomb.

So where does one look?

It had always puzzled me why if one works at the sharp point of a profession throughout one's career, using the assumptions that a fresh dimension in clinical expertise would continue to become available and the past could be left behind, the political and financial worlds are always uncertain quantities. Today's position is that money is no longer in the hands of businesses but in the hands of financial corporations. And what is their purpose in life?

Workers see money in the millions and billions being paid out in global deals, every day. They see predators and off-shore untaxable havens for wealth, so they naturally feel they ought to share in the fruit, with more money to spend themselves. They see vast handouts of money by countries which are themselves heavily in debt. So handouts look like currying favour. And someone has to consider the national debt, or federal deficit.

My senior partners developed ideas which were 50 years ahead of their time. Thinking and inspiration were a daily pursuit. Our personal credits did not count. For example, the commonest method of general anaesthesia today was invented by Sir Ivan Magill fifty years ago. Only his specialist friends today remember his name and commemorate it with an annual award. He was an adopted uncle of mine.

It took me a further 30 years to discover the explanation of the failure of capitalism as an idea which was interested in civilisation. I was adequately prepared for this discovery when I arrived at it. Hence my hope that these notes will save the reader a lot of time.

Three phases of research observation prepared the way.

The first was the curtain lifted by a Scots scientist and theologian who stood far enough back from his research to view the accepted pattern of the progress of science and to him the obvious next dimension. He described the wholly inadequate lip service offered by so many nice people today to the meaning of life. His was the natural next step for the human race, which totally eclipsed today's confusions. His ideas had caught my imagination by the age of twenty.

The second was the very practical procedure offered by an American as a way to deal with the derailments of human nature. This opened the way to having a role in changing the course of history. His ideas caught my imagination during university years.

The third was the presentation of my own findings on how to deal with stress, against the background of so much gossip about the subject which did not deal with first principles.

At the age of 64 I decided to return to university, this time at Cambridge, as a research student. And by good fortune I had uncovered the signposts for the new route for capitalism into the future. The 'father of capitalism' had laid out the structure 200 years ago. To my, so-called, modern education: "*Adam Smith, The Wealth of Nations*" meant just these six words and no more. But that was just the start. An answer began to form to my question of why economists could make so many decisions for my life, which were so different from the orderliness of my scientific training.

My research suggests that capitalism missed the signposts right from the start. Oh, the signposts were there, but the excitement of a nation (Scotland) emerging from the aftermath of the Battle of Culloden, the break up of the clan family circle, the invention of the steam engine etc. and the beginning of factory life made it easier to make profit without the demand for time for contemplation and deep inspiration. Human nature enjoyed the thrills.

The man who alerted me to the puzzle of the failure of capitalism was an historian in the Faculty of History at the University of Cambridge, Duncan Forbes M.C.,M.A. He is an authority on 18th century Scottish thinkers.

His lectures on Adam Smith and the Scottish Enlightenment cleared the way to the obvious - capitalism and economics left out the decisive research at the heart of decision-making which Smith had begun to articulate. Smith had started the articulation of the structure of the genetic fingerprint for our nature, our personality, 200 years ago. This matched my own research writing on the subject of Stress and the importance of clear guidelines to the structure of correct decision-making, and to the structure of the anatomy of human nature. His book *The Wealth of Nations* which gave him the title of 'Father of Capitalism', was just an adjunct to his anchor work. Smith's genetic research is contained in his book *The Theory of Moral Sentiments*. It is a manual which has two targets. The first is his research into the type of person needed to live at an emerging time of great expansion, a close study of human nature. The second is his search for words to describe the very practical route through the controversial, emotional, vague area of the personality and human nature which had moral and religious dimensions, not readily pigeon-holed by practical business men.

The Theory of Moral Sentiments was written when he was 36 years old (1759). Thirty-one years later (1790) he had honed and re-designed it for publication six times.

Smith's basic thought on economics has been developed and changed to suit the changing world scene of capitalism. And there has always been the shadow of 'the invisible hand' behind the creative ideas through the ages. What has not been done is to look at Smith's basic thinking as a scientific proposition. The alarms about wars across the world, population explosion, plagues, pollution of the environment, multi-million dollar/pound debt, are not addressed as the genetic engineers dealt with the chemical structure of the D.N.A. with all of today's possibilities on offer. So, survival to eternity may not hold true any more for the human race, unless this is done.

So, why write about Adam Smith?

First, as father of capitalism, he set in motion sound ideas which we have turned into global international debts and loans. These, the nations of the world will be unable to handle, because to repay them would mean increasing personal taxation and the public will not vote into power anyone who will cut their spending power. On present form, there has to be growing chaos ahead.

Second, Adam Smith has been misinterpreted. His grand design has been by-passed by the choice of men who mistook their initiative for success to be the target for life, and failed to grasp the vital half of Smith's design. For most economists, it would appear that Smith has not yet been discovered.

I have assembled his thoughts in such a way as to enter the field of investigation of a genetic fingerprint for our nature. These I have called *Smith's Triangle* to ensure that unless all three sides are in operation, don't expect to find the full answer to problems. The idea of a grand design was in Smith's mind.

A complete change of destiny awaits disclosure and it rests in the uncovering of the true genetic fingerprint, now smudged by our human nature.

So, while we clarify our targets for life, speed the process of skill in our work, meet the challenge of technical change, we are obliged to be alert to the signals which will change the course of history, and the contribution we are individually obliged to make.

What might appear to be an additional time-consuming exercise, which we have no time for, actually produces an operative answer we may never have heard of before, which simplifies the rescue of capitalism with hard evidence in our own lives.

And Adam Smith started it while contemplating his panoramic view of 'free enterprise'. He began to articulate a new philosophy - the genetic fingerprint for our personality. Each of us is unique. He was contemplating the needs of the move from medieval life to industrial life. We are now amidst the move from industrial life to saving a crumbling civilisation.

If those who are looking beyond Lenin, as East Europe is doing now, look West, what will they see?

If Smith had been discovered, the evidence would be there in writing. Compare the tonnage of books on economics which acknowledge the basic thought of Smith's *Wealth of Nations*, and the almost entirely non-existent writing built on his *Theory of Moral Sentiments*. I am constantly astonished to learn how many eminent thinkers have never heard of it or his *Rhetoric etc*.

Smith's *Theory of Moral Sentiments* has to be called the study of new truth, even if it is 200 years since the basic research was done.

We are obliged to investigate the catalyst of our ideas.

Chapter 2
ADAM SMITH'S GRAND DESIGN

By horseback from university in Glasgow, to university in Oxford, at the age of 17. An age when success was indicated by a curled wig and gold-headed cane, not a fuel-injected/turbo engine in your car.

"AMONG the young writers these days one can observe a great deal more career ambition ... a sense of failure if they haven't made their first million by the age of 30 ... the new literary star search.

"What also seems to have departed from the world for the moment is the desire among young writers to create the masterpiece, the total work that, whether gorgeously compressed or encyclopaedically vast, seems to say all that must or can be said at its particular moment."[1]

We think things move fast today but the man who gave the correct signals before the industrial revolution, Adam Smith, went off to university at the age of 14. Three of his professors at Glasgow, Professors of Greek, Mathematics and Moral Philosophy, were already drawing students from all over Europe. It was the latter who launched the famous phrase: "the greatest happiness of the greatest number."[2] He was also the first to lecture in English and not in Latin.

Smith was a man whose target was 'the total work', a grand design.

In three years, aged 17, Smith had won a scholarship to Oxford (worth £40 per year) and was off South on horseback. However, it appears that Smith found Oxford "a place of intellectual stagnation."[3] Smith's response was to "read deeply and widely in several subjects and in many languages"[4] particularly Latin and Greek classics which were well stocked at the college, Balliol. He worked hard in the practice of translating French "to illustrate

23

the institutions, the manners and the ideas of different ages and nations."[5] His Oxford scholarship was intended for students considering the Church as a career. Smith however left Oxford and returned to his home in Kirkcaldy.

At the age of 25 he was launched by an Edinburgh intellectual impresario to give a course on English literature. Later he went to Glasgow giving "admirable lectures on language on the different kinds of characteristics of style suited to different subjects ... the proper arrangement of different members of the sentence."[6]

Aged 28, Smith stepped into the vacancy which had occurred on the death of the Professor of Logic and the illness of the Professor of Moral Philosophy at Glasgow University.

Smith had a unique style of his own. In his lectures on rhetoric and belle-lettres, he taught how to impress and persuade with self-conscious elaborate style speech. With the study of light literature he drew attention to certain gestures or the "peculiarities of dress" which indicate "something mean and low in those in whom we find them".[7] The more sophisticated can also detect class differences by the sources of language structure. He taught his students to write making language a sensible tool of analytical thought and to use short sentences to "express the thought of the author".

Today we are even instructed on how to dress to be impressive in Europe. It has become incumbent upon the representative of the British company who will 'go into Europe' to dress in the proper manner. "Will the business traveller fare well when 12 national cultures fuse together in 1992 or will sparks fly? Sceptics would reject the idea that there is such a thing as power dressing and that what you wear has any tangible effect on whether you win or lose a particular deal ... but you are what you wear ... items of clothing that will help impress the right people are:

1. Briefcase: the more expensive the better.
2. Wallet: ditto.
3. Cufflinks: no party cracker prizes allowed here.
4. Shirt: this should be the most expensive item, as a first impression is created in the first 90 seconds and only the

face and neck area are taken in ... shouldn't wear it white at all, but a softer version say oyster, ivory or soft white to enhance the looks."[8] And so on.

What would Smith have thought of it?

My impression is that Smith was launching the search for the structure needed for tomorrow's world, the structure of our creativeness. In speaking to the young he used his study of the development of Western thought to build foundations, to make certain that progress was assured. He had the patience to pick out illustrations which could linger in the mind for ever.

In the manner of an instructor, Smith discussed with his students (his Didactick manner) the need for a proposition and the great need of keeping things simple. The structure of our personality was his proposition, though yet to be defined.

"If there be but one proposition necessary to be proved, there can be nothing more simple, the best method here undoubtedly is: First, to lay down the proposition and afterwards advance the several arguments that tend to prove it, which may be summed up, or brought to conclude in the same terms as the proposition."[9]

The wonder of Smith's grand design is missed if we lose sight of Professor Mizuta's clear observation of the core of Smith's thinking: "It is his observation of individuals in society from the point of view of a moral philosopher which led him to establish a new science of political economy... Young Adam Smith as a moral philosopher is also a political economist."[10]

This is the dimension of which we appear to be fearful.

Smith's proposition is that subordinate propositions should not exceed three as the mind "cannot comprehend" more. He taught his students the first of the three parts of his grand design in his lectures on rhetoric: "Subdivisions are not at all easily remembered, they always run into confusion and become too intricate for our memory to comprehend...In the number three there is a middle and two extremes."[11] Smith does not enlarge on the possibilities of this simplification, which we were to see as the years went by.

Without declaring it, he was structuring his three propositions which would unfold his grand design: 1. His lectures on rhetoric. 2. His central concern as expressed in *The Theory of Moral Sentiments*. 3. His political economy in *Wealth of Nations*.

Today's obsession with economics makes us vulnerable to many distractions, because we fail to grasp the significance of sub-propositions 1 and 2, number two being the main proposition.

Smith's forward thrust was always based on foundation thinking. He goes right back to the early study of feelings and sentiments, for his building of a real structure for human nature, and the structure of sequences in our mind.

In his essays on philosophical subjects, the *History of Astronomy*, he begins by taking his story of outer space right back to our feelings of Wonder, Surprise and Admiration.We Wonder at the rare phenomena of nature, eclipses, plants, animals, things of which we are not acquainted.We are Surprised when we bump into a friend in a place we did not expect to meet him.We Admire a country scene we have observed a hundred times before.

The force behind these three sentiments has more influence than we have yet accepted. Smith makes a scientific observation that early warning of the above allows our nature to adjust to the coming effect. The mind, when it expects a new experience, prepares itself, although we may be quite unconscious of this. So, "without violence, pain or difficulty" the new emotion "glides gradually into the heart."[12]

But, if the event is unexpected, the effect can be violent, even cause death, by its "entire disjointing of the whole frame of imagination", the sequence of thought in our mind. Hence our thoughtfulness in warning someone that we are coming to give bad news.

There is a sudden change in the sequences in the mind when an emotion is brought upon it with the whole nature of Surprise. We are suddenly alerted to danger. This was a daily experience when the flying bombs assaulted London. One walked on pavements on the north side of the road if possible. Suddenly there would be the noise of the engine coming from the south. Two immediate reactions: where to take cover, listen for the engine to stop and cause the bomb to do its 45 degree dive. I've seen a taxi driver dive under his cab.

Smith raises the effect of two extremes, like grief and joy, succeeding each other. He cites the reconciliation after quarrels and the eruption of passionate relief. He is indicating the effect of his 'invisible hand' on the situation. "There seems to be something in the nature of Surprise which makes it unite more easily with the brisk and quick motion of joy, than with the slower and heavier movement of grief."[13]

His appreciation of the inbuilt structure of cultures is seen in his observation that those accustomed to grief are less harassed when new grief comes to them. He then puts the sentiments of grief and joy together, as labelled structures of our sentiments, a continuing picture of our impressions in the mind, the anatomy of human nature.

The mind is constantly looking ahead, as we saw with grief and joy. And when anticipated, it is less surprising: "When two objects however unalike, have often been observed to follow each other, and have constantly presented themselves to the senses in that order, they come to be connected together in the fancy, that the idea of the one seems, of its own accord, to call up and introduce that of the other... this association of ideas, becomes stricter and stricter, the habit of the imagination ... grows more and more rivetted and confirmed. As its ideas move more rapidly than external objects, it is continually running before them, and therefore anticipates, before it happens, every event which falls out according to this ordinary course of events...They fall in with the natural career of the imagination."

"There is no break, no stop, no gap, no interval." The coherent chain of ideas floats through the mind of its own accord, "without obligation to assert itself."[14] This constant sequence is only interrupted when the order is not the same. When there is an unfilled gap. A horse eats grass and it grows flesh and bones – how?

Smith is looking upon imagination as a practical structure. He points to the interruptions in easy flow of thinking and suggests we get behind the scene, the physiology of how the above happens. This is Smith's orderly route to mature thinking.

Getting behind the scenes in the study of the sun, moon and stars then unfolds in his story of the philosophers of astronomy through the ages.

Today we have to remember that Smith is talking about thinkers, as men who had a grasp of all that was known of human knowledge, in all subjects, not our analyst/expert/consultant in the small areas of life we label today.

He puts it: "Philosophy is the science of the connecting principles. Nature, after the largest experience that common observation can acquire, seems to abound with events which appear solitary and incoherent with all that go for them...Philosophy, by representing the invisible chains which bind together all these disjointed objects, endeavours to introduce order into this chaos of jarring discordant appearances..."[15]

What would Smith think of philosophy today? Lack of training in real philosophical method has produced today's immature professional man, people like myself who are dedicated to their disciplines, fascinated and isolated.

"Philosophy, real philosophy" says Roger Scruton, "is burdened with a great task of restitution."

Smith's courtesy in laying out the support for his proposition, is illustrated by his suggestion of looking at the method of Socrates: "Keep as far from the main point to be proved as possible, bringing the audience by slow and imperceptible degree to the thing to be proved, and by gaining their consent to some things, whose tendency they can't discover, we force them at last either to deny what they had before agreed to, or to grant validity of the conclusion...This is the smoother and most engaging manner."[16]

At all times when he is teaching the young, Smith is building for them the art of being straightforward. He illustrates this from classical Greek and Roman times. He infers that if you were to read the works of Aristotle's *Ethics* or any other of his works ten times over: "you would hardly have a notion of a plan." Even if Aristotle intended to avoid confusion, the plan is there.

The need to be uncomplicated is another of the strengths of Smith's design. The words we use should be born of our own language. The changing style of speech over the period of his own life was as today. He comments on the "good old English word *Unfold*", which was "thrust out of common use by a French word of not half the strength or significance to wit, *Develope*." "The word can never convey the idea so strongly to an English reader." "*Insufferable*, expresses our emotion and indignation at the cruelty and oppression of a tyrant, while *intollerable* means only that there is some difficulty and uneasiness in supporting the heat of the sun." [17]

Smith's wisdom about the impression we make on others causes him to suggest we use short sentences when writing and be "so plain that one half asleep may carry the sense along with him."[18] And whatever is most interesting in the sentence, on which the rest depends, should be placed first. He is constantly saying that your mind and spirit is what comes across, whatever you say. He does however allow 'a tail' to come at the end of a sentence to hold the mind in suspense.

The freshness of Smith's approach is there, as he warns that we think of forefathers as "much soberer and grave, solemn sort of people than we are".[19] So everything about them gives the idea of gravity and solemnity. He is keen we use metaphor to build "allusion betwixt one object and another" – intellectual and corporeal or the mix of them. These are used to "give due strength of expression to the object described" as in "the bloom of youth" "the fields rejoice and were glad."

He warns however, that "bombast" and "burlesque" can as easily happen. Again training his young audience, using past thinkers he quotes Milton (*Paradise Lost*), "When he compares the grating of hell gates to the thunder, the metaphor is just, but if he had compared the noise of the gates of a city to thunder, the metaphor would not have been so just...and still less if to the door of a private house." Mixed metaphors must never run together: "bravely arm ourselves and stem the sea of troubles."[20]

Hyperbole is important to Smith: "To say that a man is a mile high would not be admired as a lofty expression; but when Virgil compares the two Heros, Turnus and Æneas coming to battle, to two large mountains, the grandeur of the two objects is suitable to each other."[21]

When Smith constantly repeats that: "The style of an author is generally of the same stamp as their character", he is beginning to outline the deeper search of the structure of personality: "he should regulate that character and manner that is natural to him and hinder it from running into that vicious extreme to which he is most inclined." Write, says Smith to "... remedy inaccuracy or partiality of former writers ... to grasp the differences between magnifying events to stir the emotions and narrating the facts in as interesting way as possible with impartiality."[22]

Again training the young in expressing themselves, he quotes from Addison, illustrating his modesty of character: "he delivers his sentiments in the least assuming manner and this would incline him rather to narrate what he had seen and heard, than to deliver his opinions in his own person." He is concerned that a man becomes "agreeable company. ..when his sentiments appear to be naturally expressed."[23]

Smith begins to underline the difference between the two ways of dealing with discourse. The first puts forward the arguments on both sides of the question in their true light, giving each its proper degree of influence, and has it in view to persuade no further than the arguments themselves appear convincing, the 'Didactick'. The other endeavours by all means to persuade us, and for this purpose magnifies all the arguments on one side and diminishes or conceals those that might be brought on the side contrary to that which it is designed that we should favour, the 'Rhetoricall'.

Persuasion, which is the primary design in the latter, is but the secondary design in the former.

When Virgil describes "the tumbling of a torrent down a Rock he strengthens the Picture by describing a traveller astonished and surprised on hearing it below him."[24] And again: "descriptions should be short and not taedious by its length."[25]

Another of Smith's important markers is his description of the 'tinctures' which add to our character. "It is not so much the degree of Virtue or Vice, probity or dishonesty, Courage or Timidity that form the distinguishing part of a character, as the tinctures which these several parts have received in forming his character." "Men do not differ so much in the degrees of Virtue and Wisdom as in the other Ingredients of their character." [26]

To describe a man's character, says Smith, requires "great skill, deep penetration, an accurate observation and almost perfect knowledge of men." Here he is beginning to declare his belief that every single person is unique. Or as Frank Buchman used to put it: "Reading men."

The indirect description is related to the effect it produces on the outward behaviour and conduct, and we can be so general in our descriptions that "they exhibit no Idea at all".

Proper observation is necessary of the "more complex and important actions of men". The impressions which we chiefly use, says Smith, are those of the unfortunate kind and those perceptions of uneasiness. Again he draws his students' attention to detail by saying that the artist painting the portrait of Agamemnon could not by all his skill express a degree of grief suitable to what then filled the breast, so: "He thought it more prudent therefore to throw a veil over his face." Even comedy needs the "cross accidents" which threaten an unfortunate end.

All this attention to the detail of man's feelings accumulates as the structure of his human nature.

Taking Smith's instruction to heart, "historical writing ... sets before us the more interesting and important events of human life, points out the causes by which these events were brought about ... and the manner and method in which we may produce similar good effects."[27]

He makes plain the necessity to give reason for the events which happened before the principal event, to dispel curiosity. A look at how Smith arrived at the foundation thinking for the work which labelled him 'father of capitalism' is essential, if modern political science is to interpret him correctly. And the 'principal event' must surely be the definition of the genetic fingerprint of personality, so well prepared in *The Theory of Moral Sentiments*. Today's headlines in the daily press might read: *The Dawn Raiders of the Stock Exchange,*

The Taxing Questions for the Offshore Predators, The Cash In on the Treasure Trove/Bonanza of more than £1 billion, all portend a different picture from that which Smith was constructing.

Smith wanted his listeners to grasp the difference between magnifying events to stir the emotions and narrating the facts in as interesting a way as possible with impartiality. There should be no gaps in the unfolding of a story with clear truths, which make a lasting impression.

Continuing his training of the student of his day, Smith constantly used illustration from the Classic writers, to build up the sequence of events. Poets came first with hymns of honour, military exploits, themes about great men, then fairies and monsters. Then the beginning of prose writing with Herodotus with his writing designed to amuse, rather than instruct; Thucydides with his subject, the history of a war; then Xenophon with a less strict style; and on to Polybius, giving "the Civill constitution of the Romans, rendered not only instructing but agreeable."[28] Latin historians come next with Livy as the best. His sentences, says Smith, are always very short: "the first sentence implies all the following ones."[29]

Smith continues to build his theme: "that the incidents of private life, tho' not so important, would affect us more deeply and interest us more than those of a Publick Nature." When describing a national conflict, Tacitus "leads us so far into the sentiments and mind of the actors that they are some of the most striking and interesting passages to be met with in any history." All of these points are directed to his prime concern for "internal causes" leading us into "a science no less useful ... the knowledge of the motives by which men act, a science too that could not be learned." In other words, there is little chance of understanding motives in other people, unless we have looked at our own seriously, and related them to the conflicts around ourselves.

A further look at our human nature shows our servility towards those superior to us and our inhumanity to our inferiors. We can laugh at them and not weep at their misfortune. Smith underlines the common idea that if we exhibit good nature and humanity we are often timid and lack attack. He is clear that men prefer to be great than good. And again he uses the word "tincture" to suggest that character is influenced by the family and friends around us.

He continues to plot the development of human thought by making military art the most important for the Greeks, then games and music. He makes the point that philosophy did not begin in the heartland of Greece, but in the colonies. He describes how Gorgias introduced eloquence to Greece, as the wealth and opulence of Greece developed.

He could be describing the search for knowledge today. As wealth expands, one surface sign of it is the surge of country establishments fitted as conference centres, with attractive leisure facilities. Professional journals have massive lists of post-graduate courses and credit is given by the National Health Service for attending some of them.

Smith continues to build up the picture with the deliberative orations of Greek classic orators whose "spritely language" aimed to excite the Athenians to go to war with vigour, and to the Latin language of Roman Cicero, which was more grave and solemn, yet possessed of "a very high degree of sensibility ...", the change from warfaring enterprise, to citizens on an equal footing, with the growth of familiarity between the lives of the population.

"Demosthenes and Cicero both adapted to the state of their country," says Smith. He did not, when he implied the further dimension of the invisible hand.

Smith (almost for fun) brings his young audience up to date: "The Lords in their speeches to one another always observe the same rules of Decorum and if any thing of passion be hinted at, it must be hinted only. We see that those who have made great figures as speakers in the house of Commons, where a very loose manner is admitted of, lost their character when transferred into the upper house."[30] He suggests they were not able to lay aside their former manner.

Smith has touched on foundation ideas, yet all the time we sense the birth of his challenge.

We may think that research in outer space, gene

engineering, information technology has brought an undreamed of change to the world scene. Just as dramatic a change took place in Smith's time. It is important to relate the industrial changes to those who attempt to give an economic interpretation of history. They have attempted to explain all the processes of life as mechanical procedures. The profit motive was emphasised to the point where it seemed to intensify the selfishness of man. Entrepreneurs came into existence. With the fast development in the use of steel, coal and transport, more and more factories were launched. Canals and waterways were built to hasten the speed of factory production.

Britain led the way with her command of the seas and the setting up of colonies all over the world. These provided raw materials for the factories and when converted into saleable goods, for a good export bounty paid by the government. Much land was used for factory buildings and more and more people left the country for work in the now crowded towns. For 100 years Britain was political leader of the Western world. Smith's writing was beginning to be appreciated by thinking men. Prime Minister Pitt in a typical remark: "We will all stand till you are seated, for we are all your scholars."[31] A European view of him at that time: "Next to Napoleon, he is now the mightiest monarch in Europe." His thinking was in parallel with America's Declaration of Independence of Thomas Jefferson (1776): "Constitutional democracy in its modern sense was born as a twin of the market economy." But both Constitutional Democracy and the Market Economy have a fresh challenge. We have, over the years chosen parts of Smith's strategy to suit our 'free enterprise' and have not looked at the warp and woof of his requirements for the life of the man of the future.

POSTSCRIPT

We will not understand the real humility and shrewdness of Smith unless we have at least a glimpse of his private life - how he thought for other people and the Scotland of his day.

The committed mind

It is always worth remembering the joy all of his research must have given him. If an idea came to mind during his 'chicken broth', he would stop playing the card game enjoyed during eating, he would forget everyone and attend to his new idea. He is reputed to have walked 13 miles in his dressing gown, deep in thought, before realising the situation.

Lady Mary Coke (February 1767) wrote to her sister stating that Sir Gilbert Elliott mentioned that Mr.Damer had paid Smith a visit a few mornings before. As he was sitting down to breakfast, falling into discourse, Smith took a piece of bread and butter, and, after rolling it round and round, put it into the teapot and poured the water upon it. Shortly after, he poured out a cup and on tasting it declared that it was the worst tea he had ever met with. "I had not least doubt of it," said Mr. Damer, "for you made it of bread and butter, instead of tea."[32]

His Printer

His toil of writing, the 25-hour day, the attention to detail, mark his analyses as shrewd. To his printer (William Strahan), just before the fifth edition of *Moral Sentiments* was published, he wrote: "I think it is predestined that I shall never write a letter to you; except to ask some favour of you or to put you to some trouble. This letter is not to depart from the style of all the rest. I am a subscriber for Watts (steam engine) copying machine. The price is six Guineas for the machine and five shillings for the packing box. I should be glad too if he could send me a ream of the copying Paper, together with all the other specimens of Ink etc., which commonly accompany the Machine........ should there be any remnant......pay it to my tailor...He is a very honest man."[33]

This commitment goes right back to the first edition of *Moral Sentiments*. He had not replied to a letter to someone associated with his printer: "Tell him I have not forgot what I promised him but have been excessively hurried. My delay will occasion him no inconvenienancy: if it does I shall be excessively concerned and shall order some papers I left in England to be given to him. They are not what I would wish them, but I had rather suffer a little repudiation with the public as let him suffer by any negligence."[34]

At the start of this letter his sharp eye fell on the pages of the book called to question: "My Dear Strahan, The opposite leaf will set before your eyes the manifold sins and iniquities you have been guilty of in printing my book. The first six, at least the first, third and fourth and sixth are what you call sins against the holy Ghost which cannot upon any account be pardoned. The Remainder are capable of remission in case of repentance, humiliation and contrition. I should have sent you them sooner. (The following SIX Errata must be corrected as totally disfiguring the sense. Errata TWENTYFIVE of less consequence.)"[35]

The advice of learned friends

Smith paid attention to learned friends who offered criticism of his work (an important habit for all who wish to contribute to serious thought).

Gilbert Elliot of Minto, 3rd Bt (Keeper of the Signet) offered an alternative view to Smith's on moral judgement. Smith replied: "I thought myselfe infinitely obliged to you for the objection which you made to a Part of my system... I thought it would be better to alter... to obviate that objection... This cost me more time and thought than you could well imagine the composition of three sheets of Paper would stand me: for nothing is more difficult than to insert something into the middle of what is already composed and to connect it cleverly at both ends."[36]

In support of his anchor theme, in the middle of the pages he returned, he wrote: "The weak, the vain and the frivolous, indeed, may be mortified by the most groundless Censure or elated by the most absurd applause. Such persons are not accustomed to consult the judge within concerning the opinion which they ought to form of their own conduct. This inmate of the breast, this Substitute for the Deity, whom nature has appointed the Supreme arbitor of all their actions is seldome appealed to by them. They are contented with the decision of the inferior tribunal. The approbation of their companions, of the particular persons whom they have lived and conversed with, has generally been the ultimate object of all their wishes. If they Succeed in this, their Joy is compleat; and if they fail they are entirely disappointed. They never think of appealing to the Superior court."[37]

Smith kept in stride with the most forward thinking of his day. To everyone, young and old, thinker and student, printer and reader, he offered standards.

Adam Smith's Scotland

The most devastating prelude to the Industrial Revolution was the effect which the move from medieval society had on people. In the past, employer and employee worked together on a common task. As the birth of industry gained momentum, the intimacy was lost. Employer and employee had to change their habits. They had become pieces of a process which would be judged primarily by profits.

By the time Adam Smith was 37 and had just published the *Theory of Moral Sentiments*, labourers in Britain were in a state of subjection to conditions near to slavery. Before Watt and his 'complicated' steam engines, a child of twelve working in a factory might do 10 to 14 hours per day. Further, as children went off to work, home life changed and parents did not exert their authority as before. The Industrial Revolution weakened the moral teaching in the schools and in the church.

Instead of a family unit or organisation which had economic and moral authority, industry made the company the unit of production. There was the loss of the discipline of the parents, teaching co-operation and moral character. The sequel to this was that as machines were introduced and child labour became unprofitable in the factories, children became economic liabilities. There followed a longer period in the life of a young person before he could be self-suporting. That gap made further difficulties with moral codes which had been a customary part of country life on the farm.

The old moral code was dying, claim the historians, and a new one had not been formed. The hunger for education was intense.

The speed and dimension of change matches our own today.

Number Thirteen

Gentlemen,

We have received your Letter of the 16th Instant, inclosing a Return of Seizures No 249 by the Collector's Clerk for three & an ullage Anker of Rum & a Box of Tea; And previous to settling the distribution of this Seizure we direct you to report in whose possession the Swine House was where the Tea was found & what share of this Seizure should be allowed, also to transmit to us such Proof as can be got for ascertaining that the Persons ment in the Return were concerned in the landing & depositing the two Ankers found among the whins.

We are,

Your Loving Friends,

Adam Smith

James Edgar

Rob Hepburn

Custom House, Edinburgh 21 January 1790. (Property of Kirkcaldy Museum and Art Gallery, Andrea Kerr, Curator.)

Chapter 3

SMITH/SOCRATES : THEIR FUNDAMENTAL R and D.

Smith's research picks out Socrates' search for something beyond knowledge and the very special nature in every one of us. Smith, like Socrates, was a pivotal figure in history.

ADAM Smith's full offering has not been developed and enhanced, because we do not stand back often enough to view the marvel of the maturing of civilisation and our precise role therein.

Whatever we feel about the latest method of selling 'our product', or satisfying our creative instincts, or the need of finance, we rarely accept that any fault in such a process has anything to do with how we live.

The following eight questions refer to Smith's fellow explorer of thought, Socrates:

How many of us are condemned to death because our fresh thinking challenges the methods of national policy (in the West)?

How many look forward to discussing where civilisation has got to, with eminent thinkers, (long dead)?

How many set out to be a midwife of the mind, by talk which brings to birth the 'interlocutors' thoughts'?

How many have an inner voice which warns them when to do or not to do things?

How many discover that the mind rather than material force sets the universe in motion?

How many enjoy the founding fable of democracy, when two gifts were sent to earth to help men live in amity – not just the gift of being a shoemaker or a physician, given to a few people, but the gift of shame and respect for others, given to everyone (Zeus to Hermes)?

How many have spotted the first exercise of free speech by a commoner or the debut of totalitarianism?

How many would claim they differed from their contemporaries in wisdom only because they are aware, as their contemporaries are not, of the total extent of their own ignorance?

Adam Smith's close attention to the development of civilisation naturally attracted him to this pivotal figure in history. Socrates was the man who started the whole question of defining what we mean by this and that. He was laying down the first bricks in the structure of definition.

Like Smith, Socrates was looking towards the leadership of the future. In 400 B.C. this resulted in Socrates having a following of young sons of the rich, who had the time to listen to him. He taught them rhetoric and logic, to challenge the aristocracy of Greece. Socrates was a catalyst for making men think and these young men took to civil war, because they saw the conflicts in Athens' government. They fancied taking on leadership themselves. Socrates' principal accuser at his trial (Anytus) was really against him because of the battle for the education of his son.

Greece was not a free society. Courts were manned by half-mad juries of 500 (said Aristophanes) and trying cases was like a public meeting, with professional informers (sycophants) out for gain. Socrates' young followers were men who had money to buy the weapons to force three 'political earthquake' periods of dictatorship (oligarchy) on Greece during his own lifetime.It is against that background we see Smith as a catalyst challenging us to think deeper than economics and the law of the land.

Socrates' search for knowledge was not in line with the democracy of his day, initiated by the lawgiver and social reformer Solon, 200 years earlier, that everyone should be able to sit in government: the joiner, the physician, the ship's captain. Socrates was not for this system of government. He proposed that a man be found "who really knows", a "shepherd of the flock". He said that if the government wanted advice on building, it could ask a joiner etc., but advice on governing the country is not a gift of the craftsman.

Like Smith, Socrates was searching for the motivation

behind man's thinking. He called it virtue and soon suggested that it should be possible to describe these feelings.

Three themes were central to his thinking:

1. Something beyond democracy, amidst much class war and no true freedom of speech.
2. The search for virtue as something teachable, like knowledge.
3. The search for something beyond 'polis' (general Athenian government) which had to do with the soul.

But his young men, now dictators (Critias and Charmides), did not want more citizens to be educated in the art of thinking taught by Socrates which could prepare them for government. They told him they had changed the law and he could not go on with his philosophical teaching.

It is worth seeing how he dealt with his 'young dictators'.

Socrates did a piece of philosophical reasoning with them: "Do you think that the art of words (techne logon) from which you bid me abstain, is associated with sound or unsound reasoning? For if with sound, then clearly I must abstain from sound reasoning; but if with unsound, clearly I must try to reason soundly." Charmides became very angry: "You may not hold any converse (dialegesthai) whatever with the young." "Well then" said Socrates: "that there may be no question raised about my obedience, please fix the age limit below which a man is to be accounted young." Charmides: "You shall not converse with anyone who is under thirty." Socrates: "Suppose I want to buy something, am I not even to ask the price if the seller is under thirty?" Charmides: "Oh yes, but you are in the habit of asking questions to which you know the answer, so that is what you are not to do".[1]

His trial was really a political occasion and the charge of impiety – not respecting the gods (gold, silver, etc.) worshipped by Athens; worshipping strange deities of his own and corrupting the youth of the city was a sham to get around the amnesty at that time in the dictatorships .[2] It is unlikely that the court would have taken kindly to Socrates' assurance that he had an inner voice which told him when not to do things.

I.F.Stone in his book on *The Trial of Socrates* offers what Socrates might have said: "Ideas are not as fragile as men. They cannot be made to drink hemlock. My ideas and my example will survive me. But the good name of Athens will wear a stain for ever." Stone records: "Socrates appears to be the first Greek to speak of the psyche (soul) as the seat of knowledge and ignorance, goodness and badness, 'not to care for your bodies but for the protection of your souls'".[3]

Smith knew that the Christian message had not yet arrived on the scene in Greece and that gods (small g) were everywhere. He had read the stories like the one about the disastrous battle in the Peloponnesian war, when Athenian General Nicias set up a secret attack on an unprepared enemy (Syracuse), but just as everything was ready to go and none of the enemy was on watch, there was an eclipse of the moon. This was 'a great terror' to the general. He quaked at the sight and called off the assault, a prelude to the greatest Athenian disaster of the wars. The general was ignorant. He understood that disbelief in the supernatural and the teaching of astronomy were indictable offences.

Athens in the fifth century B.C. was an open market for ideas over many years. This is reflected in Acts 17, when St.Paul visited the city over 400 years later and taught the message of Christ risen from the dead. The Greek inquisitive mind did not throw him out of the city but suggested "we listen to this idea further". "You bring some strange things to our ears, we wish to know therefore what these things mean".[4] Plato, the recorder of Socrates' words, was responsible for St.Augustine being led to believe in Christ: "having gotten the hint from Plato, about the search for incorporeal truth".[5]

Smith's *Theory of Moral Sentiments* picks out Socrates' search for something beyond knowledge. He underlines the acceptance of an *Impartial Spectator*: "Amidst the respectful admiration of his followers and disciples, amidst the universal applause of the public, after the oracle (a message divinely inspired) the wisest of men, the great wisdom of Socrates, though it did not suffer him to fancy himself a God, yet was not great enough to hinder him from fancying that he had secret and frequent intimations from some invisible and divine Being".[6] He is referring to Socrates' inner voice, his Daimonion.[7]

Smith however suggests that "the religion and manners of modern times (1759) give our great men little encouragement to fancy themselves either Gods or even Prophets. Success, however, joined to great popular favour, has often so far turned the heads of the greatest of them, as to make them ascribe to themselves both an importance and an ability beyond what they really possessed ... precipitated themselves into many vast and sometimes ruinous adventures".[8]

In the line of history, Smith upholds Socrates' majesty of the sensitivity of the heart of the human race, its magnanimity: "Whenever we meet with any examples of such heroic magnanimity, we are always extremely affected. We are more apt to weep and shed tears for such as seem to feel nothing for themselves, than for those who give way to all the weakness of sorrow ... the friends of Socrates all wept when he drank the last potion (of hemlock) while he himself expressed the gayest and most cheerful tranquillity".[9]

Smith begins to point toward the object of this work, the very special nature of everyone and in what the *structure of that personality* consists. The structure of excellence as seen by Socrates,[10] "By the wise contrivance of the Author of Nature, virtue (observance of standards of right conduct) is upon all occasions ... the surest and readiest means of obtaining both safety and advantage ... The surest way of obtaining the advantageous judgement and avoiding unfavourable judgement of others is to render ourselves objects of the former and not of the latter. 'Do you desire' said Socrates 'the reputation of a great musician? The only sure way of obtaining it is to become a good Musician .. General .. Statesman ...'".[11]

If Smith had aimed to find a basic description of life lived with the *answer to the modern misconception of stress*, he could not have chosen a better one than the words of Socrates: "The heroes of ancient and modern history, who are remembered with the most peculiar favour and affection, are, many of them, those who, in the cause of truth, liberty and justice, have perished upon the scaffold, and who behaved there with ease and dignity which became them. Had the enemies of Socrates suffered him to die quietly in his bed, the glory even of that great philosopher might possibly never have acquired that dazzling splendour in which it has been held in all succeeding ages".[12]

To his accusers he said: "If you put me to death, you will not easily find another, who, to use a rather absurd expression, attaches himself to the city as a gadfly to a horse ... a 'sluggish' horse, which needs a bit of 'stinging' for its good".[13]

The Athens of Socrates' day chose to claim 'freedom of speech', but did not have the rule of law, so was not a free society.[14]

Smith had much to feed his grand design in his excursions through the thinking of Socrates and many other Classic scholars. It has much significance today.

Chapter 4
ADAM SMITH'S DISCOVERY

Smith searches the anatomy of human nature, the structure of our individual personality. He uncovers the key to the decision-making process.

BY the age of 36, Smith had constructed what was his first observations on the nature of man, in his book which had taken him ten years to write, *The Theory of Moral Sentiments*. He laid down what would later become the basis of the three requirements for today:
1. The triangle of thought needed to come up with the correct answers: Smith's Triangle.
2. The uncovering of the genetic fingerprint, not only the chemical one of the D.N.A., but the genetic fingerprint for each personality.
3. The resolution of conflict between the multi-cultures of the world, taking mankind on to the next plateau.

Smith moved in the same way as today's genetic engineers and microbiologists move. As a hardheaded Scot he penetrated the complex motives of human life. His language was amusing and lucid:

"People of the same trade seldom meet together, even for merryment and diversion, but the conversation ends in a conspiracy against the public in some contrivance to raise prices."

"Most of our money is spent on things which are not necessities."

"People model behaviour so that they are approved."

"It is vanity which interests us, not ease or pleasure."

"Why are ordinary persons benevolent, as well as self-interested? (The butcher wants to be paid, but he may dive into the water to save you.)" "There is a human fascination with the workings of machines, gadgets, 'systems'. This prompts us to much hard work to the point of obsession, not the necessity of meeting our basic requirements."

Smith highlighted motives as a central area for investigation. Everyone is familiar with the word 'pressure'. Everyone uses the word 'stress' or an equivalent word. Smith might have said that stress holds the key to a fresh and rewarding future. Stress is not going to go away and I suggest that we have the wrong idea about that word. What most people mean when they use the word is strain, and in time breakdown.

We are all confronted, minute by minute, with choices and selection in our decision-making. Perhaps the oft repeated, well worn story of MacDougall will illustrate:

MacDougall was proceeding home one night from work in the little town of Kirkintilloch. Weary, he stopped off at the local tavern for a drink. After several, he suddenly remembered his wife was expecting him early. The short cut home was through the graveyard. It was dusk. He did not notice the new-dug grave and fell in. Slightly stunned, he fell asleep. Next morning the local factory hooter went: "Toot!" "Toot!" He wakened. Looked up. Saw where he was and said: "My God! It's the Last Trump!" He climbed out and looked around the graveyard and said: "My God! What a poor turn out for Kirkintilloch!"

MacDougall was derailed a long time before he fell into the grave. Sometime toward the end of his work, when he was subconsciously spinning the computer of his decision-making process, a few more facts had been fed in to the computer. Facts he had not paid attention to.

Now whether it was the attraction of the latest gossip he would get there at the 'local' or the pretty bar-maid, who knows? The know-how of his decision-making process was simply over-ruled by his motives and derailment was inevitable. He should have been going home.

As we have indicated, it is this pre-decision-making part of the mind where choice and selection take place. There are always two components: How to do the job – our know how. What we are in it for – our motives.

Decision-making is at the pivotal point of the rat race. The pacesetters of today are not the men of information technology. They just make things go faster. What really matters is what we do with the information they provide.

Smith was unique in his realistic appraisal of the basic requirements. His mind did not just envisage experimental science/steam engine creation/factories in embryo. He looked at ourselves, the people who were to live in that glorious/ambitious/propulsive future which he could not have imagined at that time.

Yes, Smith was searching at a wholly different level.

He was well aware of the fast expansion of the export market. One of the fastest ways of making money was to exploit the government bounty offered for export. The shipment was loaded, government bounty paid, the ship sailed off to a neighbouring port and off-loaded, re-load, second bounty paid and so on.

It wasn't a Porsche then; it was the scarlet cloak, curled wig, cocked hat, gold headed cane, and 'equipage' (coach, horses and footmen) seen around the streets of Glasgow.

He had more to say about the training of the young. Foreign travel usually resulted in them returning home "unprincipled, dissipated, incapable of serious application to study or business."

In fact, my guide into the thinking of Adam Smith put it that the classic view of Smith "will not do". "People look down the wrong end of the telescope today when they consider Smith." Behind all the words and comment, Duncan Forbes showed Smith as a clear thinker who had several basic thoughts: my impressions of his picture of Smith were that:

1. He was stating general principles for whole nations.
2. You need to take a hard-headed view of human nature.
3. The rat-race is part of nature's plan. The only people who see that nature is thereby deceiving them are those who are NOT in the rat-race, e.g. philosophers. They know this is not the road to happiness, but, fortunately, it doesn't make any odds to Nature's plan. Smith takes a neutral view.
4. Improved social situations do not mean people are happier or improve morally.
5. The self-interested pursuit of commerce is, in the light of all Smith's work, only one side of the picture, or even

an abstraction from the social whole. It won't do as an end in itself.

6. There is a higher tribunal than the self-enclosed *individual* man, who, again, outside society, is an abstraction.

How much more accurate could Smith have been when he said that men are so delighted with the means to their ends, they think of this as an end in itself? Running a good business is not the end, it is just the means, the opportunity for greater responsibility. We get overtaken by our specialities.

Smith was beginning to articulate a fact which has never seriously been taken to its logical conclusion about the role of capitalism in the development of civilisation.

"The man whose public spirit is prompted altogether by humanity and benevolence, will respect the established powers and privileges even of individuals, and still more those of the great orders and societies, into which the state is divided... When he cannot conquer the rooted prejudices of the people by reason and persuasion, he will not attempt to subdue them by force... The man of system, is apt to be very wise in his own conceit; and is often so enamoured with the supposed beauty of his own ideal plan of government, that he cannot suffer the smallest deviation from any part of it.

"He seems to imagine that he can arrange the different members of a great society with as much ease as the hand arranges the different pieces upon the chess-board. He does not consider that the pieces upon the chess-board have no other principle of motion besides that which the hand impresses upon them; but that, in the great chess-board of human society, every single piece has a principle of motion of its own, altogether different from that which the legislature might chuse to impress upon it."[1]

This is an immensely important observation: every single person is different.

Smith lived personally as though he meant what he was talking about. When he left the Chair of Moral Philosophy at Glasgow to tutor the Duke of Buccleuch for three years, he made a point of paying back to each student a sum relevant to the lectures he would not be giving to them. Their response was that they had been more than compensated for the expense, by the experience of the lectures they had received. It was 'a general cry' of pleasure. The outreach of this infectious character was displayed when he helped James Watt to obtain facilities in the university to do his research in the design of his steam engine.

Smith's view was that human nature becomes lop-sided following the social disintegration which accompanies commercial progress.

Smith's *Theory of Moral Sentiments* marks out what he considers part of the structure of human nature.
Four aspects among many, are highlighted:
1. Ambition.
2. Self-importance and conceit.
3. What makes the decisions?
4. Small minds.

Ambition:

The strongest of our natural desires is to be believed, the desire to persuade. For Smith the greatest instrument of ambition is speech.

Smith asks what is the purpose of our pursuit of wealth, power, pre-eminence? Is it to supply the necessities of life? We spend the greater part of what we make on conveniences. Beyond that we are always examining those better off than ourselves. And if ambition has got 'possession of the breast' it 'will admit neither a rival or a successor.'

And this possession can mean that being accustomed to, or even to hope for public admiration will result in our nature going sour on other pleasures. What's more, the exercise of these attributes often results in the disturbance of society.

Smith bluntly says that the 'candidate for fortune' frequently abandons the paths of virtue. He may well get into a position where he can cover up the foul way he got there. Candidates can get themselves into a position above the law and not be called to question.

Smith however is always in search of the real man behind his compelling initiative. Besides the hazards of choice in our decision-making he underlines the power available when we are honest: "frankness and openness" build "confidence". We trust the man who seems willing to trust us. We relax and are glad to be guided and directed by him.

The "harmony of minds" is a thought of great power, offered by him – just like musical instruments. But it doesn't work without "free communication", and this means honesty at the very "bosom". "No man can fail to please who is absolutely honest, and it does not matter how imperfect the views expressed." Smith calls upon the high qualities of our nature, not to degenerate into "impertinent curiosity".

His depth of investigation differentiates praiseworthiness and love of praise. Though they resemble one another, are connected, often blend with one another they "are yet, in many respects, distinct and independent of one another."

Our self-importance and conceit.

Could it be summed up better in fewer words? "What most of all charms us in our benefactor, is the concern between his sentiments and our own. We are delighted to find a person who values ourselves, and distinguishes us from the rest of mankind, with the attention not unlike that with which we distinguish ourselves. To maintain in him these agreeable and flattering sentiments, is one of the chief ends proposed by the returns we are disposed to make to him."[2]

Yes, how do I make an impression on the other fellow? Is it slick dress, praising something in him from the start, the P.R.business, or are we meeting him because that is where we are meant to be at that time?

Smith all along threads through his thinking the need to change our position. This must have been what caught the imagination of his students. "To the selfish and original passions of human nature, the loss or gain of a very small interest of our own, appears to be of vastly more importance, excites a much more passionate joy or sorrow, a much more ardent desire or aversion, than the greatest concern of another with whom we have no particular connection... Before we can make any proper comparison of these opposite interests, we must change our position. We must view them, neither from our own place nor yet from his, neither with our own eyes nor yet from his, but from the place and with the eyes of a third person, who has no particular connection with either, and who judges with impartiality between us."[3]

The very importance of what should be called 'the art of reading people' is presented by Smith in a masterly fashion. "It is from our disposition to admire, and consequently to imitate, the rich and the great, that they are enabled to set, or to lead what is called the fashion. Their dress is the fashionable dress; the language of their conversation, the fashionable style; their air and deportment, the fashionable behaviour. Even their vices and follies are fashionable; and the greater part of men are proud to imitate and resemble them in the very qualities which dishonour and degrade them."[4]

Reading people is one of the basic requirements if we are to remove the barriers of a multi-culture world, looking for the real person behind the eyes. And answering the question: "What is he really living for?"

Smith is looking toward the new man needed to take his age into the future. He is obviously enlisting the imagination of his students on the equipment for streamlining their lives: "How many people ruin themselves by laying out money on trinkets of frivolous utility? What pleases these lovers of toys is not so much the utility, as the aptness of the machines which are fitted to promote it. All their pockets are stuffed with little conveniences. They contrive new pockets, unknown in the clothes of other people, in order to carry a greater number."[5] (I think he must have been forecasting the modern golf bag.)

What makes the decisions?

Most minds are like Catherine wheels in full and active glory. They are alive with molecules of thought called *notions*. There are so many of them they are like clouds. They bump into each other as they whizz around. They are described as small round structures with just a tiny projection which is made to fit and lock on to certain other particles of thought possessing similar projector/receptors. Most of the time nothing comes of this confused activity. How well we know this feeling.

When we are feeling alert, reacting to some event, there is more chance that there will be more projections likely to touch. It is only this outside projection which counts for docking. When two meet and lock this becomes a very small *memory*. It is estimated that after that, the joined pair do not whizz around but travel in a straight line. They meet other pairs of notions and begin to look like *live organisms*. Soon they look like shellfish on the sea bed, covered with other notions, however varied and not really similar. This mass of notions shifts to the centre of the mind, with an orbit of its own, rotating slowly now. It has become an *idea*.

For a moment this idea can attract everything in the mind and just as suddenly the centre fails to hold and all is lost. "There is a black hole," says cancer research worker Lewis Thomas. But on the other hand all these orbiting ideas may well harmonise with each other and we are nearing *the process of thinking*.

The meticulously ordered dance of ideas, with streamers and plumes of thought, picking up other conglomerates can put the mind into *a single structure*; an over-brief description of the flurry of notions started by every look and thought, sound and smell.

Adam Smith began to describe this process of the mix of the vague feelings in the mind, the time when we have some say in what we think about, and the final outcome in the way we live. He introduces the passions which 'drive' and those which 'seduce'.

"The man who acts according to the rules of perfect prudence, of strict justice, and of proper benevolence, may be said to be perfectly virtuous. But the most perfect knowledge of those rules will not alone enable him to act in this manner: his own passions are very apt to mislead him; sometimes to drive him and sometimes to seduce him to violate all the rules which he himself, in all his sober and cool hours, approves of. The most perfect knowledge, if it is not supported by the most perfect self-command, will not always enable him to do his duty.

"Some of the best of the ancient moralists seem to have considered those passions as divided into two different classes: first, into those which it requires a considerable exertion of self-command to restrain even for a single moment; and second, into those which it is easy to restrain even for a single moment, or even for a short period of time; but which, by their continual and almost incessant solicitations, are, in the course of a life, very apt to mislead into greater deviations."

It is this investigation of the pre-decision-making area of the mind which marks Smith out as a man who has been harshly treated by the 'free enterprisers' who did not take his basic thinking seriously.

Smith goes on to say that the most perfect knowledge, if it is not supported by the most perfect self-command, will not always enable us to do our duty and we become ashamed of ourselves.

He may have recalled the old testament story of King David, who was a sensitive person, lamenting the death of his friends Saul and Jonathan, pictured in Handel's *Dead March in Saul* but open to Smith's portrayal of the weakness of incessant solicitations of moral temptation.

As my Cambridge theological advisor puts it, he calls attention to Old Testament II Samuel Chapter 1: "This is a sad blot on the escutcheon of King David. Why did he do it? We have no answer to this question but we can see how it happened. Sin begins in small ways as it always does, and unless checked at once leads to disaster. It was a warm night in early spring and David could not sleep. He ascended to the flat roof of his house to refresh himself with the cool evening air and saw a woman washing herself. He looked again. It is said any man may look at a woman – it is the second look that is sinful. And so it was with David. He sent for her with the result that she became pregnant. This was serious as she was a married woman. Her husband is Uriah, one of the soldiers of David. David gave orders that he is to be placed in danger in the next engagement and then abandoned. This is done and Uriah is killed. What started as a look has ended in murder. David then took her to wife. But the thing that David had done displeased the Lord. David confesses his sin to Nathan, is forgiven but the punishment remains."

Our small minds

Smith rubs in the smallness of our minds and our self concerns. He writes about the very little interest we take in the great concerns of our neighbours.

"Let us suppose that the great empire of China, with all its myriads of inhabitants, was suddenly swallowed up by an earthquake and let us consider how a man of humanity in Europe, who had no sort of connection with that part of the world, would be affected upon receiving intelligence of this dreadful calamity... He would, I imagine, first of all, express very great sorrow for the misfortune of that unhappy people, he would make many melancholy reflections upon the precariousness of human life and the vanity of all the labours of man, which could thus be annihilated in a moment ... speculation ... effects upon the commerce of Europe, trade and business of the world in general ... when all this fine philosophy was over ... humane sentiments expressed ... he would pursue his business, pleasure, repose, diversion ... as if no such accident had happened." On the contrary: "the most frivolous disaster which could befall himself would occasion a more real disturbance."[6]

SMITH'S RESEARCH MARKERS

Free enterprise has a background theme which looks toward 'the invisible hand' as the nearest it can get to a relationship with an ill-defined purpose for civilisation. It is hoped that by giving people a chance to harness their personal initiative, they will automatically help everyone else.

"Every individual necessarily labours to render the annual revenue of the society as great as he can. He generally, indeed, neither intends to promote the public interest, nor knows how much he is promoting it ... he intends only his own gain and he is ... led by an invisible hand to promote an end which has no part of his intention."

Smith now begins his labelling of what he sees as the structure of this invisible hand.

"No man during either the whole of his life, or that of any considerable part of it, ever trod steadily and uniformly in the paths of prudence, of justice, or of proper beneficience, whose conduct was not primarily directed by a regard to the sentiments of the supposed impartial spectator, of the great inmate of the breast, the great judge and arbiter of conduct.

"If in the course of the day we have swerved in any respect from the rules which he prescribes to us, exceeded or relaxed our frugality, exceeded or relaxed on our industry, if through passion or inadvertency, we have hurt in any respect the interest or happiness of our neighbour ... it is this inmate who in the evenings, calls us to account for all those omissions and violations, and his reproaches often make us blush inwardly both for our folly and inattention to our own happiness, and for our still greater indifference and inattention, perhaps, to that of other people."[7]

"The man of real constancy and firmness, the wise and just man who has been thoroughly bred in the great school of self-command, in the bustle and business of the world, exposed perhaps to the violence and injustice of faction, and to the hardships and hazards of war, maintains this control of his passive feelings upon all occasions ... He has never dared to forget for one moment the judgement which the impartial spectator would pass upon his sentiments and conduct. He has never dared to suffer the man within the breast to be absent one moment from his attention ... He does not merely affect the sentiments of the impartial spectator. He really adopts them. He almost identifies himself with, he almost becomes himself that impartial spectator, and scarce even feels but as that great arbiter of his conduct directs him to feel."[8]

Smith's picture of the Impartial Spectator widens. He teaches the further requirement of developing our values: "The all-wise Author of Nature has, in his manner, taught man to respect the sentiments and judgements of his brethren, to be more or less pleased when they approve of his conduct, and to be more or less hurt when they disapprove of it. He has made man, if I may say so, the immediate judge of mankind and has, in this respect, as in many others, created him after his own image, and appointed him viceregent upon earth, to superintend the behaviour of his brethren..." while allowing them "the tribunal of their own consciences."[9]

Smith challenges our values further, when he almost prophesies the fashion which will be at the core of economics so many years later, the 'credit card' life: "The man who lives within his income, is naturally contented with his station, which, by continual, though small accumulations, is growing better and better every day. He is able gradually to relax, both in the rigour of his parsimony and in the severity of his application. ... the prudent man is always both supported and rewarded by the entire approbation of the impartial spectator, and of the representative of the impartial spectator, the man within the breast."[10]

Smith began to be precise about moral standards. "It belongs to our moral faculties to determine when the ear ought to be soothed, when the eye ought to be indulged, when the taste ought either to be indulged or restrained. What is agreeable to our moral faculties is fit, and right, and proper to be done, the contrary, wrong, unfit, and improper.

"Since these, therefore, were plainly intended to be the governing principles of human nature, the rules which they prescribe are to be regarded as the commands and laws of the Deity, promulgated by those viceregents which he has thus set up within us, ... general rules ... what are properly called laws ... to direct the conduct of his subjects.[11]

"By acting according to the dictates of our moral faculties, we necessarily pursue the most effectual means for promoting the happiness of mankind and may therefore be said, in some sense, to co-operate with the Deity, and to advance as far as is in our power the Plan of Providence. By acting otherwise, on the contrary, we seem to obstruct, in some measure, the scheme which the Author of Nature has established for the happiness and perfection of the world and to declare ourselves, if I may say so, in some measure, the enemies of God."[12]

As I read *The Theory of Moral Sentiments* there unfolded at least one pattern in Smith's thinking. There could be discerned a group of ideas which described our *Initiative*, another which outlined the structure of our

Values and a third which clearly signalled the introduction of *The Impartial Spectator*. Here then, was a measure for decision-making, which matched the search in my own work on Stress over the years. Here then, was the beginning of the resolution of the constant uncertainty about Capitalism. The Impartial Spectator is no longer a neutral onlooker, but the Author of Nature, God. (These have been given capital letters, as he does, as they begin to label Smith's new structure.)

Here then, was *Smith's Triangle*. It said boldly: unless all three sides are in operation, don't expect the right answers.

However splendid 'the good guys' who feel called to lead nations, when do we hear about the search for the direction of The Impartial Spectator? Any day on television we may see our major political leaders attending a memorial service in church. They look correctly serious in this setting and it can be assumed that they believe in God. If so, then the Lord's Prayer is their belief and in it are the words: "Thy will be done on Earth." How then do we get four/five wills in the House of Commons, and power to the strongest? No problem then for the divisive forces to operate, with the support of the media.

"From whence, then, arises the emulation which runs through all the different ranks of men, and what are the advantages which we propose by that great purpose of human life which we call bettering our condition?"[13] – our *Initiative*.

"In the same manner, to the selfish and original passions of human nature, the loss or gain of a very small interest of our own, appears to be of vastly more importance...than the greatest concern of another with whom we have no particular connection. His interests... can never be put into the balance with their own, how ruinous soever to him. Before we can make any proper comparison of these opposite interests, we must change our position... We must view them...with the eyes of a third person."[14]- our *Values*.

"But though man has...been rendered the immediate judge of mankind, he has been rendered so only in the first instance; and an appeal lies from the sentence to a much higher tribunal,...to the man within the breast, the great judge and arbitor of their conduct."[15] – *The Impartial Spectator.*

What has not been examined is the corollary to Smith's evidence. If there are blockages to the growth of these elements, then the full personality is not uncovered. Could it then be proposed that this structure is as unique and precise as the chemical structure of the physical (D.N.A.) body?

The implications of the discovery of the chemical uniqueness of every single person have yet to be realised. They are global in outreach. If every personality is unique as well, and we learn to pay attention to the Impartial Spectator with as much enthusiasm as we do our skills, the world implications can change the course of history. We have three elements in this fingerprint of ours: *Initiative, Values, the Impartial Spectator.* – the *I.V.I.S fingerprint* of our personality.

This is the basic structure of Adam Smith's Grand Design. It's global prospects are unlimited and we are obliged to start with ourselves.

The stimulating flashes we have of the advance in genetic engineering and the view of the universe from a space-located telescope, suggest that man's mind has a vast area available for exploring *what we are* and *where we are.*

Research in the dimension of *who we are* is long overdue. The constant argument in social and political life indicates the inadequacy of our search for the future. We are meant to uncover the plateau beyond the physical imagination of man.

We need overarching turths which apply to the cultures of the whole world. Smith's IVIS is one of them. We leave the past behind.

Chapter 5

BREAKING THROUGH TO SMITH'S THINKING

"The reading of it necessarily requires so much attention and the public is disposed to give it so little that I shall still doubt for some time of its being at first very popular"[1].

THE size of the wall to be broken through should be made clear. According to John Kenneth Galbraith, no economist has offered so much range of thought. "His lengthy digressions are worth the interruptions. He had four canons: 1. Taxes should be predictable. 2. Collection should be at the convenience of the taxpayer. 3. Cost of collection to be a modest part of the total. 4. Subjects to contribute to the state in proportion to ability."

It is however important to make it clear that among such eminent economists today, obsessed with 'free enterprise' and the force of initiative there is a typical outlook: "there are three books you can quote from without having read them: The Bible, Das Capital, Wealth of Nations." I quote from Galbraith's own words: "Adam Smith, not to put too fine an edge on matters, was Scotland's greatest son. Wealth of Nations is his greatest and almost his only book."[2]

This is not so!

When the liberal thinker only uses half of the evidence from which he measures/constructs his wisdom, a serious result is produced. The modern vast expansion of computer knowledge, which the human mind cannot cope with except as individual specialities, requires a different filter for decision-making.

Professor Bernard Williams put it in his recent B.B.C. talks on *truth*: "These programmes render us the service of release from the supine admiration of computers. Many stand in awe of these repetitive toys because they are supposed to have 'memories' potentially equal to man. What they have, a learned colleague confirms, is simply storage space. Memory is not a series of pigeonholes from which we draw information at will, it is more like archeological shards (notch, chunk, fragment) from which we reconstruct our own truths about the Universe and about ourselves."[3]

Smith could not have imagined the development of organisations which ceased to be subordinate to the market. They had access to all the capital they fancied, fixed prices, sought out supplies and influenced consumers, a power not different from that of the state. He could not have forecast the pride people could have in their organisation. Corporate interest did not coincide with the public interest, as the Smithian system assumed. With increase in private consumption has gone an increased demand for public services, provided by the state. In Europe the nation-states have created the ultimate monument to Adam Smith, the European Economic Community. In even more specific tribute to Smith – the Common Market.

One has to recall that the public sector barely existed in Smith's day. Taxes existed to pay for the armed forces and a minimal government machine and that was all.

Today, the Rt.Hon.John Major MP, reflects on the 70 year hold of Marxist economics in the world and continues: "The fact that Eastern bloc countries are beginning to introduce free market policies is the clearest indication that the planned economies of socialism are in retreat. It is not necessary for political philosophies to prove that free enterprise economics are superior to planned economies. History has done that and the political judgement of Eastern Europe is starting to endorse it. Their people too have observed that political freedom and economic freedom are indivisible."

He goes on: "The simplest and most effective way to subject public enterprise to the invisible hand (of Adam Smith) is of course by privatisation."[4] This means that the privatised/public services need to be run by men who have taken Smith's fundamental lessons to heart and applied the formula of the Impartial Spectator, with its central requirement of the will and design of the Author of Nature. This was not done when the entrepreneurs and impressarios of Smith's day let their initiative have full charge of their mind.

Today we have just as global a change ahead of us, when we consider today's surge of world cultures, which are behind many of the conflicts which portray a great uncertainty for the future.

John Major is right in drawing attention to the invisible hand. It has a pivotal role in whether this civilisation survives: "I do not believe that incentive means financial reward alone ... individuals enjoy greater job satisfaction and perform better ... efficiency and better service come together." Smith's assertion that every single one of us is different gives real hope to anyone that he can give a new meaning to the word entrepreneur. Major quotes an assessor of Smith: "He never engaged in any sort of trade and would probably never have made sixpence if he had."

Smith was a man whose core truths were sympathy, insight and understanding. His Grand Design shines through all the time.

The Rt.Hon.Nicholas Ridley MP, picks out the content of a man's character: "Smith based his thought – his economic and social thought on his perception of the psychology of man. He believed that man is endowed with certain faculties (reason and imagination) and particular propensities (self-love and fellow-feeling) which incline him both to the social state and at the same time are potentially disruptive of it ... Smith develops the idea of propriety and moral behaviour ... the desire to be worthy of approval of others, this creates self-restraint – a sort of internal discipline on individual behaviour."[5]

Ridley wisely called to view "another strong facet of human nature is the power of self-interest against the interests of other people. Smith said 'This self-deceit, this fatal weakness of mankind is a source of half the disorders of human life.' If we saw ourselves in the light in which others see us or in which they would see us if they knew all, a reformation would generally be unavoidable."

Or as Robert Burns, Scots poet and friend of Smith put it: "Oh, would some power the gift to give us, to see ourselves as others see us."(in English). And in his rhyming epistle to James Tennant of Glenconner:

> Auld comrade dear and brither sinner
> How's a' the folk about Glen Connor?
> How do you this eastlin wind
> That's like to blaw a body blind?
> For me my faculties are frozen
> My dearest member nearly dozened,
> I've sent you here to Johnie Simpson
> twa sage philosophers to glimpse on:
> Smith with his sympathetic feeling
> and Reed, to common sense appealing.
> "An enquiry into the human understanding."
> (Thos. Reid D.D.)

In further support of his clear conviction about *The Moral Case for the Free Market*, Ridley underlines Smith's determined "anti- romanticism", and the difference between 'the rhetoric and the reality'. Smith is "much more subtle than is often credited." And in line with the author's research into the need for personal freedom, Ridley says: "Before we can proselytise in Eastern Europe, we need to proclaim the moral basis of the free market society here at home."

The Rt. Hon. Malcolm Rifkind Q.C. M.P., calls it the search for "a higher philosophical plane."

Two thinkers of today make it startlingly clear that a dramatic shift of the size of Smith's 18th century is with us.

Sir James Goldsmith fills in the background when he says that the world population at the time of Smith was 900 millions; today it is swollen to 5 billion and may be 11 billion by the end of the next century. He adds that the intervening years since Smith have seen industrial change which has severely damaged our planet.[6]

Jean-Francois Revel starts his book *How Democracies Perish* thus: "Democracy may, after all, turn out to have been a historical accident, a brief parenthesis that is closing before our eyes... Democracy is by its very nature turned inward. Its vocation is the patient and realistic improvement of life in a community. Communism, on the other hand, necessarily looks outward because it is a failed society and is incapable of engendering a viable one."[7]

Goldsmith's real concern as with Smith is, what has happened to people. The effect of world conquest in its full dimension, ranging from the colonialism of European countries all over the world, to the more recent strategy by the Soviet Union of world control, has been to attempt to change the cultural diversity which abounds.

It is a dimension which matters, to accept that every single person is different and that groups all over the world have their very own culture. Goldsmith rightly highlights what was done often with the best intentions by people with conviction about their own hopes for the world. On cultural diversity Goldsmith says: "The beliefs of others which may seem bizarre, might contain some wisdoms we are unable to perceive." "It has always been my conviction that cultural imperialism is more deeply harmful than territorial expansion. The Conquistadores plundered, raped and returned to their homelands. They caused pain and injury. But the long term consequences of their actions cannot be compared to the damage caused by their successors – the proselytizers. Often, with the best intentions, they robbed whole nations of their language, religion and identity. It should not be forgotten that one man's missionary is another man's spy. When the Communists sent their proselytizers to the West to convert us to Communism, we called them spies or agents of influence. When we sent ours to Africa to convert Africans to our religions, we called them educators or missionaries. Seldom do we recognise that when we intervene and change the cultures of others, we destabilise them because we tear them away from their traditions. Deracinated they tend to drift to urban slums and sink into a slum culture." "Primal religions... account for the religious outlook of a significant proportion of the peoples of the world. They interpret man's role in a different way to that of the religions of modern Western man."

That is thinking in the dimension of Adam Smith. But it misses the entire core of Smith's proposition. The 'communist agents' are loaded with ideas aimed to destroy the Impartial Spectator. They are committed to the Leninist target of making a new man by force. And since the idea is a failure, they can turn to the Western countries, which are not committed to a programme of making a new man, and ask for help without a change of target.

The 'religious agents' gave care, medicine, education and a hope of growth in the understanding of the Author of Nature. They too have yet to do the basic thinking of Adam Smith, which aims to train us in walking with the Impartial Spectator, people of all faiths and no faith.

Our varied cultures are no longer at risk, as the grand design of Smith unfolds.

Jean-Francois Revel's book, *How Democracies Perish*, is required reading. His opening remark about democracy being possibly a brief parenthesis, closing before our eyes, suggests that today's capitalism is vulnerable to all the claims/rights of every individual. This would be a hallmark sentence if we had no serious research thinkers around.

Revel in his Paris Notebook,[8] writes on the struggle between totalitarianism and democracy: "What is at stake in that confrontation goes far beyond the purely political sphere of a simple rivalry of interests and power; it is a question of human nature, the meaning of existence and its values – in short, the entire ethical sphere." Earlier, Revel observed[9]: "But could that system...have been imposed for so long upon one-third of mankind unless some secret kernel of totalitarianism lay at the heart of every human being?" (He is referring to the same book mentioned at the outset: *Cogs in the Soviet Wheel* by Michael Heller) And in his conclusion about research: "Creation, in the scientific domain as in others, is necessarily the extension of what is known – 'experimental science does not set out to explain the unknown in terms of the known' – the truly new and promising fields of investigation are those whose existence no one suspects."

These wise men are anticipating the headlines for the works to be written. Smith was giving structure to human nature. A sense of failure is a most essential starting point, to be followed by the memory of fresh discoveries we have already experienced and which do not have to be explained. Then there is the reassurance that the next conviction will be as surely constructed for us.

It is very important to remember when examining any illustration of evil – and the blockages (i.e. what is still missing from Smith's I.V.I.S., Initiative, Values, Impartial Spectator, genetic fingerprint,) have to be labelled evil – that it is NOT evil men we are examining. The fact that some appear to employ evil methods, means that they themselves have learned to exploit weaknesses in other people. Or they do it because they are ignorant that the force of evil is in possession of their own minds. Smith was interested in the weakness in the human mind and the needed nourishment.

We pick up reactions to events locally, often without evaluating them. They become our private point of view. We build assumptions often in ignorance of all the facts, again Smith's valid point about understanding other people. You can always give encouragement to the people you meet, by encouraging them to make the experiment that each is a very special person. And they sense this quality in you, sense authority and are immediately encouraged.

One might hear a sermon from the pulpit of a Presbyterian church in Scotland, that the Catholics are 'not of God' (My personal experience). Or we see on television thousands of Muslims, head down to the ground in prayer, while their 'clan' wars wreck a piece of the world.

If we need further stimulation to pursue Smith's challenge, there is a piece in Elias Chacour's book *Blood Brothers*.[10] A Palestinian reports: "For Isaiah, in his long testimony, made it amply clear that God was requiring a true change of heart in the Jewish people, a change in their traditional exclusiveness which caused them to believe that they alone were God's favoured ones. All the prophets had made it clear that such thinking led to pride and error and wrong-doing." "God's Israel included 'foreigners', those who were not of the fleshly tribes of Israel, but who had been grafted into his family, just as the branches had been grafted into this fig tree."

Never for a moment should the commitment of those who do not want Smith's proposition to be searched be forgotten. It is reported that there exists a powerful lobby of scientists both in the U.S.A. and in Britain who campaign against any research being conducted on genetic differences among human beings. This New Left assault on science caused a department of our British Museum (Natural History) London, to be closed in February 1985.[11]

One has to be aware of subliminal penetration of the mind. Roger Scruton describes it: "Linguistic emancipation means shooting your mouth off in a world where everyone has an equal opportunity to do the same ... untrammelled yapping." New filters to the mind develop as we pay attention to the real targets behind much of today's attempts to influence us.

"We look up at the sky and see stars as they were light years ago ... We need to match ourselves for the most fascinating hour in the greatest human drama ... One of the main tricks of the devil is to keep us paralysed by fear of our own shortcomings, instead of mobilised by the power of the living Christ."[12]

Adam Smith's grand design is not complicated. To understand it, we do not have to be educated in the foundation thinking of Classical Greece, nor the cell biology of biomedicine, nor the rhetoric of the academic mind. The authority of the Impartial Spectator shines out and penetrates. The urgency of giving structure to Smith's Triangle, his Genetic Code, is the responsibility of successful people in every walk of life. The real practical meaning of the guidance of God, call it what we will, is not the privilege of one section of the community. The challenge is to work at articulating that experience so that others will catch the power of it.

PART II
THE SMITHIAN SEARCH

W here does the Smithian Search take us? As each of us has a unique fingerprint of personality (I.V.I.S), everyone has a unique story to tell.

Four earlier stages of search have been recorded by this Smithian searcher.

The first, while at the age of twenty, I have called the *Galactic Dimension of Adam Smith.*

The second, while a medical student, I have called *Beyond the 'Market' and the 'Gene'- Smith's challenge*

The third as a junior assistant in private practice, I have called *Modern Surgery – Taking Smith's Proposition Seriously.*

The fourth comes from my own research into today's rat race of specialists, I have called *Smith's Grand Design for the Stress of Life.*

Finally, I have reflected on the need for all front runners to accept that 200 years ago Adam Smith was laying down, not just a structure for free enterprise, which, through the years has been developed by economists galore, but a need to accept that his Grand Design contained much of the foundation thinking required now and merits the title of the text for a new philosophy, *A Global Writ on Offer.*

As I said at the outset, I was introduced to Smith after all these exercises of search and I am sad that thinkers these past 200 years did not make the time to go on building a Smithian hard-headed view of life as a whole.

Fortunately, government Ministers today are articulating these, beyond Party, requirements for the future. And without Smith's suggestions we will be hard-pressed to find the language which will by-pass the narrow self-inflicted views of today's media out-pourings.

That is the challenge.

We have to face the fact that there was a time when there were men who could discuss all available knowledge. The speed of change has slotted us into pigeon-holes. Smith's Triangle however, begins the development of a supra-channel of exchange, which removes the self-interest at the heart of the world's dilemma. It restores a dimension which is beyond today's isolation of a myriad world cultures. We expect a daily dose of revolution from the media. As a colleague, an Oxford intellect, wrote me: "One remembers that both the Russian revolution and the French revolution moved from the end of tyranny to a new and harsher tyranny. It took France 40 years to move to stability and when one remembers that none of the East Europe lands have ever known any kind of democracy and Germany itself has only been more or less a united country for 70 years, let alone a stable democracy, one has to stop and think. It is the height of folly to suppose that Germany has the same current of thought as we have."

The West has a sizeable task on hand. With all our experience of democracy, we can rise to it.

Chapter 6

THE GALACTIC DIMENSION OF ADAM SMITH

One hundred years ago the Channel Tunnel promoters were headlined in The Times, 1 January 1890. One man lifted the curtain on a totally different dimension needed to satisfy the human mind.

IT is wise to pursue a hero of early life. Find out what he thought and did. John Buchan, the author of a long list of vigorous adventure stories started to pour them out from the age of 35. The film 'The Thirty Nine Steps' is based on one of the books. He became Director of Information during World War I and later Governor General of Canada. His adventure stories filled in the landscape over one period of my questioning of life around the age of 20.

Shortly after, I began the 'discovery' of Henry Drummond. Here was a scientist with an exploring mind which appeared to use his science training to make him search for much wider perspectives.

He was born in 1851 and lived for just 44 years. 100 years ago, the problems of the country differed little from the present ones. Uncertainty in the nation. The Channel Tunnel. The Irish Question. The state of our roadways.

The London Times of Monday 17 February 1890: "Change is the first law of the universe and restlessness is a primary condition of improvement. Nothing could be more pernicious for any community as that its leaders should be content to leave it exactly where it was. From this point of view all friends of humanity ought to rejoice at the commencement of every Parliamentary Session. It

69

is only necessary to glance at the notices for leave to bring in Bills to be assured that the whole nation is in a perpetual state of the healthiest dissatisfaction."

The London Times of Wednesday 1 January 1890, in its third Leader, puts it: "The promoters of the projected Channel Tunnel have again deposited their Bill to the Private Bills office, and the Board of Trade has again intimated that it will be the duty of the Government, as on previous occasions, to oppose it in Parliament."

Here we are at 1990, and the tunnel?

The need for thinking at the level of Smith is underlined in the leader in The Times of Wednesday 28 January 1880 page 9: "The Duke of Marlborough has declined to accept the hospitality of the Lord Mayor of Dublin at the annual Civic Banquet to be held on the 3rd of next month... All things considered, it is perhaps unfortunate that the abstract Viceroy of Ireland should be unable to dine with the abstract Lord Mayor of Dublin... The Prime Minister of England has never found any difficulty in accepting the hospitality of the Lord Mayor of London on Lord Mayor's Day, though the official chief of the City may have been his vehement opponent in Parliament...It would be a new Irish grievance at once if we were to hint that Irishmen were unable to attain to the pitch of abstraction which has long ago been pronounced to be within the reach of Englishmen."

In contrast, the debate among ordinary citizens is amusing: third Leader, The Times, Thursday 9 January 1889 reads: "... we have lately published, and continue today, a series of letters containing very conflicting opinions on the subject of the best material for town pavements, especially for such as are subject to the wear and tear of enormous traffic. The controversy has, so far, been confined to the relative merits of granite, wood and asphalte. On this apparently simple question the views of different persons are absolutely irreconcilable. The Managing Director of the Express Dairy Company, who should surely be in a position to speak from practical experience, says that among the horses of the company there are not, on the asphalte, nearly so many falls as formerly..."; (another gentleman) "shops on the other side of Tottenham Court Road are unknown to the ladies of his family, because he will not suffer his carriage horses to travel over asphalte."

Henry Drummond was 22 when his initiative and inspiration singled him out as an articulate man of ideas, against the background of these minimum references to the troubles of his day.

His student friends wrote him up in their equivalent of *The Students Year Book:* "We watched him our fellow student and not yet twentythree, surprised by a sudden and fierce fame. Crowds of men and women in all the great cities of our land hung upon his lips, innumerable lives opened their secrets to him...the great of the land thronged him...urged by the chief statesman of our time to a political career...He passed through the trial unscathed."

His conviction was rooted deeper than political fashion. That is the hallmark of an anchor man. Drummond had the mix required today, the orderly examination of physical fact and the exploration of the ultimate requirement for research – contemplation and intuition for the next research requirement for mankind.

We do not hear about Drummond's science which elevated him to the rank of professor. We do know, from his writing, he made new sense of life for thousands across the world. Life for him was very practical and was obviously brimming over with satisfactions of all kinds with his mix of science, travel and writing in Scotland, England, North America, Australia and further.[1]

By the age of 37 he had written one of his most modern books for all the ages ahead. That text bridged the gap between the life of the successful 30-year-old and that sense of unease which we all feel about the future. Drummond had Adam Smith's grand design for the future in his book *Natural Law in the Spiritual World* – today's galactic dimension.

Here is a dip into the last chapter of the book. No speculation as far as he is concerned. Evidence is the only criterion permitted by the committed research worker.[2]

He begins by illustrating in simple terms the two dimensions which are recognised by science today. He then declares that however perfect these dimensions, the

71

chemical and the biological; the inorganic and the organic; the 'not life' and the 'alive'; a third dimension is the normal sequence to expect. He begins with a structural analysis.

Phase-contrast microscopy to the rescue (which he did not have). He uses the clearest example to describe the two known Kingdoms: the crystal of silicon from an earth sample from the Island of Arran, on the Firth of Clyde and the fairy-like design of a shell from the sea-shore on Barbados, West Indies, with its silicon as well. The second could only have been fashioned by something 'alive'.

"When examined with a pocket lens, the Arran earth is found to be full of small objects, clear as crystal, of mysterious geometry and of exquisite symmetry. The substance is silica, a natural glass. The prevailing shape is a six-sided prism capped at either end by little pyramids of consummate grace.

"When the second specimen is examined, the revelation is, if possible, more surprising. There is a vast assemblage of glassy objects built into curious forms. The material, chemically, remains the same, silicon, but the contour is entirely different. The appearance is that of a vast collection of microscopic urns, goblets and vases, each richly ornamented with small sculptured discs or perforations which are disposed over the pure white surface in regular belts and rows. Each urn is chiselled into the most faultless proportion. A vision of magic beauty.

"Judged by the standard of their beauty, there is little to choose between these two sets of objects. The cardinal difference is that they belong to different worlds. The first are crystals and belong to the dead world. The second are shells and belong to the living world.

"If we melt down the Arran earth we cannot help reproducing the pyramid and the prism. The six-sided tendency is its Law of Crystallisation, which cannot be resisted. It has nothing to do with life. If the shell be broken, no inorganic agency can build it up again.

"So far as beauty goes, the inorganic and the organic world are one. To the man of science, however, this identity of beauty signifies nothing. No fundamental distinction in Science depends upon beauty. The scientist wants an answer in terms of chemistry, are they inorganic or organic? Or in terms of biology, are they dead or living? However much they may possess in common, of material substance (silica) and beauty, they are separated from one another by a wide and unbridged gulf."

We need to remember these words: "Wide and unbridged gulf."

"Fix attention for a moment, not upon appearance, but upon possibilities, upon their relation to the future, and upon their place in evolution. The crystal has reached its ultimate stage of development. Nothing else within its kingdom can do more for it. In dealing with the shell, we are dealing with the maximum achievement of the organic world."

A crystal is a crystal is a crystal. "It is beautiful to see its design, like the tracery of the frost on the window-pane. But it can never be something more. It has no future prospects."

Drummond drew attention to the fact that beyond the mineral kingdom there emerged the biological kingdom. It started at the beginning in the primeval sludge and today we understand much about the body's immune system, cell chemistry and so forth. Something entered the story of creation. Life began.

In just the same way that 'life' in the second scientific dimension is totally different from 'not life' in the first, Drummond presents his assertion that a third dimension is there for the uncovering. Drummond challenges us to explore the Kingdom of the Spirit, beyond the organic.

He accepted that the highest development of the second or biological dimension is demonstrated by human resource and imagination today. However, he goes on to look at the top end of this second kingdom, as he calls it, He describes the mixture in the life of 'respectable' man. He is 'esteemed', 'upstanding', lives a 'decent' life. Such lives, he continues, are lived in a mixture of moral labels and ultra-materialism.

He goes on: "In dealing with a man of fine moral character, we are dealing with the highest achievement of the organic kingdom. No matter what may be the moral uprightness of his life, the honourableness of his character, or the orthodoxy of his creed, if he exercises

the function of loving the world, that defines his world –
he belongs to the organic kingdom." So long as man's
bent is in the direction of the world, he remains a
worldling. Mild religiousness, conventional worship, traditional beliefs, living an honest life cannot begin to
savour the vista ahead.

Drummond is making it quite clear that there are no
future prospects for the man of the world. The wide and
unbridged gulf between his materialist world and this
third dimension is as clear as the divide between the first
and second scientific dimensions of matter.

"To contrast the two and marvel that the one is
apparently so little better than the other, is unscientific
and unjust." The man of Drummond's third dimension,
his spiritual man, is a mere unformed embryo hidden as
yet in his earthly chrysalis case.

What is to emerge? Drummond leaves plenty of room
for all the modern views of cell engineering, but they still
belong to the second kingdom. To attempt to live in both
camps / dimensions (the biological and spiritual) cannot
be done, says Drummond. An awkward conclusion, but
what would you expect from a shrewd research worker?

Drummond was responding to the tempo of his day,
and the need for recognition of the spiritual factor in
decision-making amidst the then ebullient industrial
revolution. His emphasis was even stronger than Smith's.

The Times, London, Monday 6 January 1890: "The
subject of profit sharing which has been discussed in our
columns for several days past by advocates and by
opponents...never has the alleged necessary conflict
between the interests of capital and of labour been more
distinctly marked than it is now, or more disastrous in its
reality. Scarcely a day passes without news of fresh
strikes...grave injury to both parties. The question of the
day is what cure is to be found for it ... common interests
of all parties. When profit sharing is promised every
workman becomes, as it were, a master. Something more
than this is needed to give permanence to the arrangement... good wages and a share of the profits cannot be
depended upon for this. The fault urged against the
system is that it weakens the allegiance of those
employed under it to the cause of labour and has even

been used with the express object of bribing workmen into disloyalty to their trade union."

"Science is beginning to waken to the momentous truth that man, the highest product of the organic kingdom, is a disappointment."

The practice of a health profession has a fundamental requirement – choosing a method of care which produces cure. We are skilled in choice. This pursuit of right answers is an orderly procedure and opens the way to a search into the whole meaning of life. Drummond penetrates this field.

"All the work of the world is merely a taking advantage of energies already there. All that man does is to put himself in the way of the wind and his sailboat moves; fixes his water wheel in the way of the stream and produces his electricity; puts his piston in the way of the steam, and holding himself in position before God's spirit, all the energies of Omnipotence course within his soul. This is a law – an instrument of scientific research, simple in its adjustments, universal in its application, infallible in its results. With the demonstration of the naturalness of the supernatural, scepticism even may come to be regarded as unscientific."

Drummond saw the development of the rule of law penetrate the misty elements of the purpose of a man's life. Man has a devouring need of liberty to shake off the failures of the past.

"Why be afraid of the third Kingdom?" says Drummond. The evolution of the biological kingdom of which we are at present a part, suggests that someone designed the Galaxy of stars, every grain of sand, every insect that lives for one hour – that dry fly on the crystal clear chalkstream.

We can be afraid for two reasons: fear of clearing the machinery i.e., the examination of all the pieces of 'our way of life' we secretly like, and the uncertainty that the route into the third dimension may not be the route we have planned for ourselves. I certainly felt that by taking my hands off my career, God might suggest I become something quite different – most alarming (I had just arrived in Harley Street aged 24).

Drummond says that when you start thinking about

God, you experience a sort of one-to-one relationship. It is a sort of private meeting. This can be alarming to the human mind. The one-to-one relationship is what any research scientist feels about his work – he and his work become one. (I felt this designing the Deep Focus Camera for Guy's Hospital.) There is a peculiar joining of ideas with the project. Drummond goes on to say that God's will is something special for the individual. At this point I am not sharing in the universal character of people in general, but something special for me, and me only.

I have moved from being a provider of clinical rules which get good results. Drummond is differentiating between those who believe in God and those who take up a career in the search for God's will for the world, irrespective of the career they follow. "A hopeless attempt to live for two kingdoms at once."

This is Drummond's most important observation.

The first lot are not, says Drummond, fulfilling God's will. No future prospects. They miss being in the counsels of God. God has something for you to do which no one else can be given to do. Few take God into their career, because they have yet to take God into their splendid successful lives. "The change of state here is not as in physics a mere change of direction, the affections directed to a new object, the will into a new channel. The change involves all this, but is something deeper. It is a change of nature." And it becomes a full-time job for which adherents naturally exclusively live and work. There is no bridge – another unbridged gulf as Drummond would say.

Of course it is popular to argue that you are no more important than anyone else. It is a hallucination of the mind to delve into these mysteries. Why not just use common sense. Just use reason, experience, circumstances, the advice of others, the welfare of others. That's the formula for any moral man. Drummond calls these "minor instruments". Helpful as they are, they are not the major instrument. It is worth recalling that there is a precise chemical structure of the D.N.A. There should be one also for our nature, as we saw with Adam Smith.

The research scientist lives with searching questions all the time. Drummond focussed on the challenge of

God's design, that there is a route through all the options and it is not via the biological dimension. He challenged us that our perspective for the world should be quite as clear as the proven practical results which give each of us authority in our chosen life work. Like Einstein he got outside the range of human thinking and reasoning and considered the laws he expected to apply to science, alongside the experience of the problems being faced by the students he taught.

His principal conclusions were that the scientific field was much, much larger than described by his colleagues in science. Many of the laws did not stop at test tubes and switches but were the same laws which passed into life in general. Drummond foresaw that the scientific approach, with its inbuilt necessity for integrity and perhaps cold-blooded evaluation, could remove from things of the spirit a vagueness which so often surrounded them and which gave them a mumbo-jumbo, pie-in-the-sky air.

As he put it: "Now that science has made the world around articulate, it speaks to religion with a two-fold purpose. It offers to corroborate Theology and in the second to purify it.... The world we live in is an unfinished world. Almost everything has yet to be done to it." "The position we have been led to take up is not that the Spiritual Laws are analogous to the Natural Laws, but that *they are the same Laws*. It is not a question of analogy but of identity."

Drummond attracted his vast audience of listeners because he suggested that there were no holds barred in the research which could turn the tide of his day and age. A new dimension was there for the experiencing. That is the Smithian grand design.

Chapter 7

BEYOND THE 'MARKET' and THE 'GENE'

Smith's challenge to thinkers.
Whether we like it or not, we are confronted
with the need for fundamental research, as
universal of application, as immediate and
commanding as Sir Ernest Rutherford's
work of splitting the atom, or Albert Ein-
stein's work on the curvature of outer space.

THEIR work was not bounded by personal, national or racial considerations. Their work was universal yet specific. They initiated a never-before-dreamed-of new world for mankind; power to launch into space and navigate through it.

Today's world has quite specific questions which we have not been trained to answer: "Who's around?"; "What are they up to?"; "What about me?"; "What's the meaning of it all?"; "Are you a scientist or are you in it for the cash?" No, not an insult but a challenge.

"How do you give encouragement to those destined to make the world's fateful decisions?" Here the thinking of such men is considered.

We know that there is a 'single key mechanism' dominating each disease. It has been uncovered time and again. Is there a factor which will move individualism beyond the totality of self-will and self-defence, to produce the great blend, like the exquisite colours of nature?

It is worth quoting from the mature thought of an eminent cancer research worker, Lewis Thomas (evaluated by Time Magazine as: "Quite possibly the best essayist on science now working in the world.").

"There is a list of around twenty-five afflictions of man in this country (USA) ... the unfinished agenda of modern biomedical science ... there has never been a period in medicine when the future has looked so bright ... For every disease there is a single key mechanism that dominates all others. If one can find it and then think one's way around it, one can control the disease ... unthinkable a half century ago ... I believe that the major diseases of human beings have become approachable biological puzzles ... ultimately solvable."

"It was clear that by simply switching off one thing ... the whole array of disordered and seemingly unrelated pathological mechanisms could be switched off, at once... I have no doubt that there will turn out to be dozens of separate influences that can launch cancer,... but I think there will turn out to be a single switch at the center of things, there for the finding."

"I cannot begin to guess at all the causes of our cultural sadness, not even the most important, but I can think of one thing that is wrong with us and eats away at us: we do not know enough about ourselves."[1]

The study of the gene is no answer to our global requirement. The molecular biologist, cellular biologist, population geneticist and the media, can make a mix suited to press headlines and can confuse or frighten us, depending on the use of words and statistics. It is clear that no learning process or information that the body receives in its lifetime can be imprinted upon our unique individual plan (the D.N.A.). You cannot teach the chemical D.N.A. anything. It passes on structure, not wisdom.

Gene engineering does not have a role in how the world will go. So the gene is old hat in terms of our global requirements.

You can add some growth hormone to the diet of the cow and it will imagine it is having more calves and will produce more milk, which of course can be useful in a country with few cows. Or you can give melatone secretion from the pineal gland and stimulate the breeding of deer. You can make them mate in the Spring and again in the Autumn, so producing twice as many females for breeding and males for meat.

These are the basic elements for manipulating life, but they do not tackle the right questions.

A colleague said to me: "Yes, I know what you are

talking about. I know little or nothing about the issues turning the world into a great uncertainty." He added: "The past fifty years are a thing of the past in clinical work." And I know that in his brief-case are a series of essential pieces of research he aims to offer in his general practice to the great benefit of his patients. And he is obviously tired. He needs refreshment for his mind. The future lies with such men.

"What is patently true is that human nature surfaces and drives people. So, without a thought for that, all Gorbachev's world challenges are faulted from the start. He has no thought on how to change human nature." This is what I wrote to one of our nation's wise men (27/1/1988) having read Gorbachev's Peristroika. I continued: "The archaeologists tell us of various civilisations which have come and gone. My mind suggests that we could become just one more of them unless we really say 'Yes' to God's will."

Next day he replied: "Yes of course our civilisation will fall. The definitive book is *Civitas Dei* by St. Augustine of Hippo, written after the fall of Rome. An equally readable (but more secular) tome, rather longer, is Arnold Toynbee's *Study of Civilisation*."

I had learned at Cambridge that many academics give you their version of some other academic's view of a third academic view of the subject you went to hear about. You still have to read the subject for yourself.

I was directed to an abridgement of Toynbee's: *A Study of History* by D.C.Somervell and reported this to my correspondent, who replied immediately: "I am glad you are tackling Toynbee."

Come March 4 I wrote again: "The attached pages are copies of the conclusions put together by Somervell on the demise of civilisation."

"How had it happened (p.910) that they had lived to see the immediately preceding generation's apparently reasonable expectations so rudely disappointed? ... a triumphantly advancing Western civilisation had now carried human progress to a point at which it could count on finding the Earthly Paradise just round the next corner.

What, exactly, had gone wrong?"

81

"If there was any validity in the writer's procedure of drawing comparisons between Hellenic history and Western (p.912), it would seem to follow ... Western society ... not immune from the possibility of a similar fate ... a possibility confronting every civilisation, including our own."

I continued with my letter: "Looking back 50 years and reflecting on Frank Buchman (the founder of Moral Re-Armament, and personal friend), the evidence against Toynbee is clearly located in his use of the word 'possibility' (not 'of course')."

"Without claiming anything, Buchman did some of the most relevant research of our time. He encouraged people to do their own evaluation of their lives, using accepted measures. Failure could be named and accepted. For myself, the urgency lay with the thought: 'Why take up God's time after I die, when I could let Him talk to me now and I could accept judgement and forgiveness?'

"This has the fascination of developing spiritual antennae, encouraging research away beyond nuclear and biological unfoldings."

Three days later the wise man replied (7.3.88): "Thank you for your comments on Toynbee. I read it in Hospital in the war and its very size and accumulated knowledge excited, and excites my vast admiration. ... For my part it seems to me that the Bible favours the unpredictable view of history."

In my reply (22.3.88) I picked out the principal themes from his letter and continued: "So, then it follows that if the Bible favours the unpredictable view of history, we cannot say that civilisation will fall. Our premises are not complete. So there is at least a third position. I think one of the magical things we have to reckon with, is that in the human body cells die all the time and new cells are being created all the time, so why not with civilisations? If my old nature can die, I could be forgiven and a new nature begin to grow. If this is so, then today is Judgement Day and I leave the past behind, all of it, and I say to God: 'I give my life to you, where do I walk now?' A great sigh of relief comes over me.

"It appears that we accept being one of the family of

82

God now. We live in total victory now: we fall flat on our face from time to time and accept that as the learning process. And if we are infectious enough, our 'disease' will be caught by others. Faith is caught, not taught."

"My observations on the subject of stress make it clear that when people get straight about the secrets of their human nature and ask God's help, He tells them what to do and they step out of the chrysalis case, to develop in the spiritual kingdom and strain and breakdown become a thing of the past. I certainly found this in many years of living and practising at 90 Harley Street. Tomorrow's world will go to those who can articulate the experience of change in human nature.

"When this is taken up seriously, this civilisation will not only NOT fall, but will do for the spiritual kingdom what the scientists have done for the biological. Gene research is necessary, but secondary to the research for tomorrow's world."

Yes, the Roman Empire did fall, but civilisation moved on with the followers of Paul.

I was inferring that so many are confused that dabbling in spiritual matters will label them as unrealistic men of the world, because 'religion' has been presented for so long as a mystical thing which has something to do with death and beyond. This has been the devil's ace card for 2,000 years. Religion concerns God's plan for the world now.

The next man who gave me direct substance to the way of having a role in changing the course of history was Dr. Frank Buchman. His research was inspired. His prime concern was that you find out all that is special about yourself. He was not interested in 'who you are, but in what you are'. He was convinced that each person was special and his concern was that we not only believe this, but expect to find the blockages to full 'specialness'.

He was automatically on your side in the discovery of the blockages in your own nature, the removal of weakness and development of strength. The range of his thinking would appeal to any research worker, investigative reporter, political economist.

The importance of this was not just that it could be a

help to remove some of the conflicts of life, but by discovery and removal of blockages, a structure of our nature, as precise and basic as that in the gene is uncovered.

As Drummond might put it: The force of evil is so steadily on the alert, that our obsession with our personal lives deprives us of experiencing the counsels of God and affecting the future of the human race.

Typical of Buchman's challenge:

"The war for the world would in future be fought out – not between countries, economics or armies, but between sets of ideas. The basic divide is between materialist ideas of left and right on the one hand and the moral and spiritual ideas at the heart of the world's great faiths on the other."

However clearly we accept this, we need to measure it against what has been fed into the minds of millions by the followers of Lenin that "the myth of God is removed from the mind of man". And Khrushchev: "We will win, but we will not have to go to war about it."

Buchman again:

"How do we save a crumbling civilisation?"[2]

"Is our academic laboratory work equal to dealing with the wear and tear of modern life?"[3]

"We are being lifted into spheres where we have not worked up to now. Are we ready for the ideological battle? No we are not."[4]

"You must dare to tread new territory, to feel your way through the thickets of convention, your own words and formulas wear thin."[5]

"In a world like this (creeds, races, cultures, workers, thinkers, drunks and swindlers) you can no longer find the way by accustomed rules and standards. It takes a new vision, a new language, a new style."

"We must learn to put our truth differently."[6]

"We need to move from breadth to depth. It's a mad world, but there is worse to come."[7]

"It doesn't matter if past ages were better or worse. We have to deal with today's world. Sin has become attractive. God must become attractive and interesting."

Buchman was challenging us to accept a fresh dimension of thought. We often excuse ourselves as not being intellectuals, we are practical men.

There are three kinds of intellectual

First, the intellectual person who would be surprised to be called an intellectual. He thinks for his own needs, his family and his life-style. He is intellectual just the same. So far, his skills in thinking have been confined to the needs of his private empire. But for some, in time of war, his thinking was jolted into a fresh dimension called 'love of country' and a whole change of pattern of life was his next experience. (I was four years down the road to successful professional life when I had to join the Army.) We face this level of change of thought today. Success in future will depend on this being accepted by us.

The second lot assume that man can run affairs. At best, they have some roots of heritage to bolster their assumptions. They rely on evidence of past experience (an inadequate guide for the future), but the expectancy of something wholly new being available does not come into their thinking. In world terms, we have today the fallacy of Soviet 'Perestroika' which says that Leninism has failed, so we need more Leninism. 'Power to the people' fails to label the fact that everyone is different and selfwill given its head will automatically make 'some more equal than others'. To have no plan for human nature is to lead millions to no answer.

The third group are the Christian intellectuals. They assume that they are filling in time until they go to Heaven, then they will make their peace with God. According to Professor Bernard Williams, Cambridge University, they are collecting green shield stamps (similar to those collected at the petrol filling station) to put on the table at Judgement Day to prove their credits. The Christian intellectual assumes that our civilisation will pass away, fall.

Buchman was seeking the development of a new type of intellectual who would pursue the finding of the uniqueness in each of us. He was not interested in starting a new movement. His core truth was: "When man listens, God speaks. When man obeys, God acts. When men change, nations change."

Buchman was clear that our task was to change the course of history by the very practical step of experience,

85

no matter how loud the voices in the media, on the platform, in the House. But how to do this? There is a sense here of the acceptance of Adam Smith's total commitment to the fruits of his research.

Chapter 8

MODERN SURGERY: TAKING SMITH'S APPROACH SERIOUSLY

We talk a lot about electronics. And we use its mechanisms without having to know how it works. But work it surely does. There are electronics of the spirit.

ANYONE who is concerned to find a new route will agree that we live a double life. Half would look splendid on a T.V. screen and the other half we would prefer not to have on screen. Anyone who is serious about finding the assured plan would agree that it would help to stop living a double life. So, take a pencil and paper and write down the details of what jumps into the mind about the events of the double life, i.e., the other half of the balance sheet. You don't have to tell anyone you are doing it. Yes, it may well take a large quantity of paper. But then, this is a serious proposition. And it is the first requirement of any research worker or explorer. He asks what is the actual situation. The enormity of our double life will only be clear to some, if this exercise is done.

It helps to make a note of the events in the past which did not live up to standards like honesty, purity, unselfishness, love.

Then you immediately argue that a lot of what has 'gone before' can NOT be put right. Okay, let us proceed.

As cancer research expert Dr. Lewis Thomas said, there is a 'single key mechanism'[1] at the pivotal point of health and disease; a place to begin the process of cure. This is always true of the body. It is equally true about this experiment, although one may not believe it. There is a single key mechanism.

Having begun by feeling that the list is impossible, there grows a sense that the situation cannot go on as it is and an experiment had better be tried. So no doubt, within the long list of 'the other half of the balance sheet' there will be the thought that something should be done about one thing.

I personally found that there were things I should do something about. I had a very good excuse for not paying my subscription to the London Scottish Rugby Club. I decided that I should pay up and tell the Treasurer why I was doing it. I was going to try out the faith of my fathers. I had no reply. There were other things to put right, difficult, but necessary.

Developing new antennae became a daily exercise. A good friend took the trouble to telephone me in the morning to get me up to spend time letting fresh thought come into my mind, before the hectic day of practice began. There developed a sense that priorities were there to see and the rest should be bypassed. I began to be aware of a fresh list of priorities. The immediate effect of this was the filtering-off of activities which were unnecessary and I did not really have time for. The charm of the guidance of morning inspiration was that there was always time for the things which needed attention. It was not the circus of keeping twenty-five balls in the air. If there was confusion there was something wrong.

Some years later I developed massive sick headaches. My wife said I looked pea-green and I could not eat and just got to work and no more. Of course my wife thought it must be her cooking which had caused this. Our wise physician asked her if I had something on my mind. Well, I had just become senior partner and I had a lot on my mind. Basically I was trying to be a 'big shot' and had stopped being myself. When this confusion of conceit and pride was accepted by me my sick headaches disappeared. I have never had another.

My conviction grew that a different approach to practice was correct. With my partner (Dr.Alastair Dow) we decided that our philosophy should be: the patient's interests must come first and cash second. Proof of the success of this philosophy added to my lectures and to three books on stress.

As the pattern of world affairs became clearer to me, while giving papers on the world lecture circuit of my profession, I decided that the power of ideology should be understood. One of my patients had been on the staff of the British Embassy in Moscow for many years. We went several times to The British Library, Colindale (Periodicals Division) where she read to me from the Soviet Journals of Medicine. Every copy had an article aimed to train the doctors in ideology. I selected some and the Library posted us photocopies to the practice. My patient would then come in and translate them to my secretary. I built up a picture of the real power of ideas and how men are trained to have an ideology, which came before all else in their lives.

Some of the neighbours will not like your research.

I decided that as I was about to become the president of an important professional society I ought to declare some of the thinking I had been doing for the future of the professional man.

The paper (presented along with Dow) was entitled: "An assessment of new factors which will decide the future of Dental Practice." The meeting was held in the Royal College of Surgeons.[2] Eighty guests sat down to dinner in the Great Hall. The paper commenced: "The purpose of this paper is to gain some perspective on the future setting in which we and our immediate successors will practice and to study some of the forces which are operative in the field... Any reasonable attempt to look into the future will of necessity include a study of the Soviet system and the dynamic idea which gives it such momentum.".... Based on thirty-six references from mostly Soviet (medical) sources the paper unfolded the manner of training, and the challenge/coercion of the professional mind to the materialist basis of Marxism... The paper then presented evidence resolving the fear of getting mixed up in religion or politics... Modern man lives in a different world, governed by different rules. The issues are not primarily political, religious or economic. They are ideological and will be decided on the basis of which ideology deals most successfully with human nature.

We continued: "One example of ideology concerns the inside story of what the London Times described as 'The Cyprus Miracle'.

"Not long ago Cyprus was the centre of interest for the whole world and in danger of becoming another Cuba on the doorstep of Europe.

"The key to the situation was the hatred and bitterness in the heart of one man, Zenon Rossides, Legal Advisor to Archbishop Makarios. The solution to this crisis began at a lunch-party held in London at which I was present. At that luncheon one Englishman faced his mistrust of the Greeks and apologised for it. He was Sir Hamilton Kerr, M.P. for Cambridge and an old friend of the Prime Minister.

"Another of Kerr's friends, John McGovern, M.P. from Clydeside, went to New York and saw Archbishop Makarios. McGovern wrote later of this meeting: 'I told the Archbishop I was not representing any nation or party and that a new spirit was needed. I said I believed a satisfactory settlement could be reached if the Archbishop were prepared to send a representative to London to talk to the British Prime Minister.'

"McGovern then left for a conference in Los Angeles. The Archbishop sent Rossides to join him there and talk further on these crucial matters. At this conference Rossides met African nationalists who had had a declared policy of elimination of the white imperialist from their countries and who had re-evaluated the situation; who now saw that it was no use removing a white imperialist if he was to be replaced by a black imperialist. The future lay with the production of incorruptible men – black and white – and that to produce incorruptible men we have to deal with human nature.

"Rossides began to understand that his own bitterness was helping to bedevil the situation in his own country. He remembered what McGovern had said to Archbishop Makarios: 'The most reactionary man in the world is the man who wants to see the world changed without being prepared to change himself first' – and he accepted this challenge.

"One of the sources of bitterness in Rossides' heart had been his belief that neither he nor his colleagues could ever get near the British Prime Minister to present the Cyprus problem as they saw it. Sir Hamilton Kerr went to Downing Street to see the Prime Minister, who at once said he would see Rossides next day... The Prime Minister asked many questions and then asked him his views on Cyprus. Rossides frankly stated that the Macmillan partition plan would not work. 'Events move so fast today' added Rossides, 'that no man is clever enough to calculate the expedient thing to do. Our only hope is to find and do what is right morally. Then events can never overtake us...'

"Rossides then put forward the ideas that eventually became the foundation of the London and Zurich Agreements."

Other illustrations were given, and the paper ended with an observation of some basic principles.

"We need to decide to pay the price in a voluntary redirection of our personal motivation for an ideology which is superior to anything the Communist or non-Communist world has yet discovered."

At the end of the paper there was interminable silence. Not even the usual polite grunt of approval or minimal clap... It was as near to a riot as I've seen at a meeting of well-heeled doctors of decorum.

I had taken the precaution of asking a colleague to propose the vote of thanks. I had forgotten to prime someone to second it ... Sir Wilfred Fish (President, The General Dental Council) got up: "I am tremendously concerned" – pause (I thought, 'Ye Gods') "that the students today should learn more than techniques at the university. They must have a liberal education at the same time. This paper may have been to half warn us of what could happen here and we might be overwhelmed."

Sir Wilfred had said at the beginng of the evening:- "Jim, if we are going to have moral re-armament tonight, I'm going home." I had replied: "When it is about to begin, I'll ring a bell, then you can leave." We both laughed.

One senior colleague came up after and said: "The only criticism I have to make about your paper is that it should have been given a long time ago. You may be too late." Sir Robert Bradlaw (Dean of the Post-Graduate School) my principal guest, said to me: "Thank you for a very courageous and interesting paper. You will have done a lot of good...."

The Council of the Society were in uproar. Indignant

New hope from Kenya

Kenya's Example

You might well ask how a film can affect the future of a country. Well, this one has. It was written and acted by Africans from all parts of the continent who had seen in Moral Re-Armament a new way for Africa. This film is called *Freedom* or Swahili *Uhuru*. My colleague, Nahashon Ngare, *together with his two friends, Stanley Kinga and Manasseh Moerane, made the long journey to show this film to my brother while he was still in detention.

"They spent seven hours with him discussing the

---

*Nahashon Ngare is a young nationlist leader, detained for five years during the Mau Mau emergency. Kinga, a municipal councillor, is an old associate of Kenyatta's and organised one of the biggest political demonstrations in the history of the country. Manasseh Moerane is editor of *The World*, the influential African daily in Johannesburg.

needs of our continent and how they could be answered. When he saw the film he urged them to put it into Swahili so that it could reach every village in East Africa.

"Since then it has been seen by over 600,000 people in Kenya, in halls, in football stadiums and in the village squares. I was one of them. The ideas portrayed in *Freedom* have completely changed my thinking and my way of life.

"The new thinking that it has brought to many parts of Kenya has played a key part in the peaceful way the elections wre conducted in the country and in preparing us for effective self-govern-ment where men of all races have an equal part to play.

THE TIMES

WEDNESDAY JULY 14 1954

Jomo Kenyatta.

letters flew about. The comfortable pursuit of personal empires had been put in disarray. I wrote to my Council: "Some people are made uncomfortable by the truth. That is their problem and not mine." The paper was reproduced in professional journals in America and Japan.

So, what about the relatively small world which is ours? There is no reason why we should fail to find the language to move our profession on to the next stage of evolution. Such wider responsibilities have yet to appear on the conference agenda.

Yes, I can hear some of the response. If the matter is one of the survival of our civilisation perhaps the successful among us will construct the new language.

There is nothing unique about looking after patients who have vast responsibilities in the nation. Several enjoyed early breakfasts in our home 'over the shop'. The following was just one contribution in the growth of stable self-government of Kenya. Lord Selwyn Lloyd (former Foreign Secretary, and Chancellor of the Exchequer) saw a film in our home which he arranged to be shown to an African Nationalist leader, then in a detention camp. The general theme illustrated that the removal of the white imperialist by a bloodbath, to be replaced by a black imperialist, would produce a situation worse than that of colonial rule. To prepare for self-government, only men trained to be incorruptible could govern well when autonomy was granted. The film was written and acted by Africans. Notice of the preparatory work appeared in *The Times*.

When Independence Day was celebrated, the Nationalist leader declared: "I want my film to be shown on television for the nation to see." He was referring to the colour film "Freedom" (translated into Swahili-"Uhuru"), he had first seen in detention. He was Jomo Kenyatta.

After this film there was no bloodshed at national elections in his country, whereas in a neighbouring land, which had turned the film down, hundreds lost their lives in election conflicts. And he attributed his own country's smooth development to the lessons the film had taught.

Frank Buchman also spoke of the *Electronics of the Spirit*.[3]

You do not have to know about electricity, nor do you

have to know where it comes from, to make use of it. Those who do not use electricity live in the dark (the other forms of light source do not match electrical sources).

"Now electronics is a new science. Spirit has been known for a long time. It's an old science. But linked with electronics, it hitches the world to a new dimension of life and thought. Millions can speedily, automatically yield to this new practice, the electronics of the spirit.

"We can scarcely grasp what the Electronics of the Spirit means. We just faintly glimpse it. Think of the veritable instantaneous reaction whereby a thought can travel across America in less than one-fiftieth of a second. And now, with electronics, in a flash you not only hear the voice but the time you speak is registered and you get the bill at the end of the month, all without any human aid. No words of mine can explain it.

"Then take the Electronics of the Spirit. It works with an Infinite Mind. It circles the globe instantly. It taps resources hitherto unexplored and forces hitherto unknown. Take the whole question of guidance – God's mind and my mind. The thought that slips in any time, day or night, can be the thought of the Author of mind. We are dealing here with facts that no one can measure.

"A thought comes – maybe just an arresting tick. One responds to it. And millions can be the richer if it is effectively carried out. It may apply to someone who crosses our path – some friend, perhaps, who may be the link which can reach cabinets, which can prevent nations from taking the wrong turning...

"We have reached a point where man must either solve his problems or be destroyed by them. Politicians in every country are begining to discover that the human mind, however able and sincere, cannot solve the problems created by the human passions of hate and greed and fear.......... How to catch this new dimension? St. Francis of Sales says the secret is to listen to the inner voice. He says that half an hour a day is a basic minimum, except when you are exceptionally busy. Then a full hour is necessary."

One of Buchman's friends adds: "What you do not write

down, you will forget. So you might as well never have thought it."

The electronics of the Spirit is not caught up in past cultures. It is as different as the change from the Chemical Kingdom to the Biological Kingdom, long and clearly accepted by science.

The 40-year-old may have to be reminded of the new dimension between France and Germany which had to be built up from scratch after World War II. France's Foreign Minister in 1949, Robert Schuman said: "In the economic field we have the Marshall Plan; in the political and military field the Atlantic Pact. Now we need to give fresh ideological content to the life of the millions of Europe... What Moral Re-Armament gives us is a philosophy of life applied in action... Democracy and her freedoms can be saved only by the quality of the people who speak in her name... Statesmen can propose far-reaching plans, but they cannot put them into effect without far-reaching changes in the hearts of people. This is the kind of work I would like to do for the rest of my life."

The new relationship between France and Germany was master-minded between Schuman and Adenauer.

Adenauer sent a message to Buchman in 1951,(reported in the New York Herald Tribune): *"Moral Re-Armament is Credited for Role in Schuman Plan Talks"*. "In recent months we have seen the conclusion, after some difficult negotiations, of important international agreements. Here Moral Re-Armament has played an invisible but effective part in bridging differences of opinion between negotiating parties... It is my conviction that men and nations cannot outwardly enjoy stable relationships until they have been inwardly prepared for them. In this respect, Moral Re-Armament has rendered great and lasting service"..."You have given most valuable stimulus to the great work of unifying Europe. I am convinced with you that unless this work is carried forward, peace in the world cannot be maintained."

We are on the threshold of vast change in Europe and the Soviet Union.

How to give perspective to committed men who are successful in their gifted lives and for whom there is little time to draw breath from the daily round. Frank Buchman on his 60th. birthday, gave me a quote from the New Testament: "Do your utmost to let God see that you at least are a sound workman, with no need to be ashamed of the way you handle the word of the truth."

People who do not apply the electronics of the spirit live in the dark. They are out of touch with the scientific knowledge now available in the universe, and who wants to be out-manoeuvered in an economics-based world? Who wants to miss adding a new technique to his skills? We have to rescue the thinkers from the philosophers. Because some people think, they are called philosophers. Most philosophers are only interested in exercising their minds on problems. In this exercise they readily keep the problem unsolved by antinomies (contradictions between two logical conclusions). Real thinkers use the scientific process and observe the unfolding of knowledge.

In the realm of thought we have now reached the area of understanding the use of the spirit in the operation of the mind. So the more we covet the skills of our mind, the more the electronics of the spirit becomes an indispensable agent in these skills. To operate without it is to work in the dark.

These stages of research are devastatingly clear as any scientist will acknowledge, evolved with the hardening of science since Darwin made absolute standards a rule.

This resolution lies with the electronics of the spirit. Buchman's work was for the mind, as the split atom is to physics. That was certainly the enhancement of Adam Smith's Triangle.

Thirty-eight years ago Moscow Radio spoke of "a universal ideology" with "the power to attract radical revolutionary minds." "Moral Re-Armament supplants the inevitable class war by the permanent struggle between good and evil... in addition to building bridge-heads on each continent and training cadres... has now started on its decisive task ... expansion ... throughout the world."

The reason why Moral Re-Armament (founded by Frank Buchman) was singled out for frontal attack by Moscow Radio, was that here was the only other group of people in the world who were not only committed to producing a new man, but they were successful at it. Buchman applied the basic triangle of thought of Adam Smith, and men around him caught the idea that God had a plan for each and every person and that the course of history could be changed.

Paul Kurowski of W. Germany[4](1989) writes:

"Anxiety about our world often comes over me. My experience of life as a worker, a communist and (later) for years a part of Frank Buchman's work and as father of a family and a happy husband are not enough to satisfy me. The idea: 'Somehow everything will turn out alright' is just not true. I know for sure, men and their governments... must be different.

"I thought of three people. One of them won half a million in a lottery, another married a superb wife and had a family. But they did not become 'different', their thinking ended – regardless of their potentialities – with themselves. The third became a convinced communist. The man changed so much that he was unrecognisable. The victory of his class in an irresistible world revolution ruled his whole being...

"I too was borne along by the communist ideology...many long years with certainty through difficult and dangerous circumstances. Many didn't understand me, but I laughed at them. But it also made me proud. ... however, in spite of my belief I began to have doubts... the difference between theory and practice...

"But all that changed totally when I met men and women working with Buchman, who showed me the completely different aims of their ideology... My thinking changed when I experienced the totality of God's absolute standards in a time of quiet reflection... Whatever a person is, Christian, atheist or materialist, black or white, rich or poor, he changes... We miss the meaning of our life if we want to remain as we are."

It is important to grasp the radical nature of Lenin's plan, because the cultural upheavals in today's world make it imperative that people understand the driving forces, and study what has happened in the past 70 years in the Soviet Union.

Lenin admitted that in spite of the successful revolution and his hopes for the success of his scientific proposition about human nature: "The machine is snatched out of your hands: it's as though there's a man sitting there driving it, but the vehicle doesn't go where it is steered but where somebody else is steering it."[5] Smith's invisible hand?

Heller points out that "no one has yet attempted to measure the destructive effect on the human organism of such permanent forms of stress as fear, chronic shortage of goods, inevitable queues, cramped accommodation, abominable public transport, innumerable prohibitions and the constant need to defy them, and a feeling of total isolation."[6]

There must obviously be a challenge to those who are not obsessed with their personal skills, who must stop in their tracks and consider that with capitalism we have freedom without a change in human nature and with homo sovieticus we have freedom being discussed and soon, the same question of change in human nature.

Could there have been the shift of power now on view within homo sovieticus, if the original fervour had not just become 'a ritual'? Does this challenge the religious labelling of the Christian and non-Communist countries? Do we perform just to a ritual?

While accepting that we live in a puff of time, there has to be the certainty that the search for a meaning to life is a daily revelation. Lenin's passion fails to feed the individual with the idea that he matters and that he matters decisively, and has his own story to tell. There is the constant upsurge of personality. The commitment to having total power over millions of people can be gauged by the presence of 325 Universities of Marxism-Leninism (1975), and 3,000 town and district schools for Party activists. The shock of the current situation must be understood. It highlights our own failure to advance Smith's Triangle.

Soviet apologist, Boris Kagarlitsky believes: "... democratic movement, striving for genuine renewal in Eastern Europe, cannot do without either Marxist theory or a revolutionary strategy"... "it is one thing to desire democracy and another to realise it in practice." [7]

Those who have made a decision of their will to pay attention to Smith's Impartial Spectator have the evidence of a power suddenly available like the splitting of the atom. Time is suddenly re-set when this happens, and this is not airy-fairy, but scientific evidence of God's availability.

As one experiences the decision to be a permanent student of the Impartial Spectator, the turmoil in the human mind can make life feel quite impossible, because the entire shift of priorities makes us feel we will look stupid to our acquaintances and rather embryonic in the new life we've decided to live. Such an experience awaits the next stage of homo sovieticus. If the mass movement for freedom from the myth of Leninism is endorsed, then just imagine the effect of millions experiencing the challenge of being honest and not obliged to conform any more to the 'rituals'. That means much sensitiveness on our part. If these millions look West what will they see? Keynes or Friedman?

The immensity of the task ahead is further illustrated by Heller, from the U.N.E.S.C.O. Annual (1981): "paper per head of the population for printing and writing: USA 65,603 kg: West Germany 51,172 kg: Japan 31,936 kg: Britain 31,794 kg: the USSR 5,117 kg."

The need for the construction of fresh language to describe the practical direction of the Impartial Spectator is essential against the background of the use of language in the Soviet Union. There are no innocent words. The value judgements have to be understood behind slogans, definitions and their real meanings. We are obliged to create language with no double meaning.

However, rooted in the Russian heritage is very real understanding of the assault on human nature. This has to be re-articulated to encourage fresh and spontaneous growth of thought. *Theophan The Recluse* revised in Russian the first principles of the spiritual combat in the book: *Unseen Warfare*. This was translated into English (Kadloubovsky & Palmer, Faber and Faber) (Theophan, Bishop, Russian Orthodox Church c.1850). Some impressions of the strategy of evil are presented:

Suppose we are successful and undertake good work in our milieu: evil just changes its tactics. We are under fire from all sides, from the front and the rear, from the right and the left, from above and below.

In front, we dream of success ahead.
Behind, we dream of our past memories.
From the right, into new undertakings.
From the left, concrete temptations.
From above, in good work which is excessive.
From below, self pity, heedlessness.

We find that evil suggests we act on our own without advice of wise colleagues. We begin to think that extraneous help is unnecessary and we preen ourselves that our success is all our own doing. The self-delusion makes us over-reach in what we try to do. Our self-esteem can cause us to have various indulgences and the illusion that we need a 'house in the sun' for rest – a little rest to the body.

We have lost our anchor which never ascribes any success, however small, to ourselves, on our own power. We have lost touch with the judgement of experienced contemporaries.One has to keep one standard in mind – evil is on the war-path and each move has to outwit it.

If we are sick, we imagine the many good deeds we could have performed if the position had been different. Evil can reverse the process and suggest to you that all your life is pleasing and successful.

Choose a place of advantage in the battle-field, and be warned of self-opinion. Talk back to your mind! ...

Theophan made it abundantly clear that conviction and strength of character had to be strong points, to compete with evil. Today's surge for freedom indicates that conviction is still present.

Adam Smith's Grand Design is revolutionary and creates permanent change. You do not follow rules, you discover the man within the breast.

Chapter 9

SMITH'S GRAND DESIGN FOR THE STRESS OF LIFE

*If we do not want to live in the dark, we do
not have to.
There is an additional piece of the formula
for decision-making to which we have
possibly never been introduced.*

THE horizons of world thinking for a profession must
go far beyond the skills of its disciplines.

My search for the route beyond clinical success was
lifted by the then most eminent man in the profession,
Dr. Harold Hillenbrand, Executive Director Emeritus,
The American Dental Association. On two of my many
visits to Chicago he spent twelve hours on each occasion,
taking me through the manuscript of one of my books on
stress. He wanted me to clarify core truths.

The following are quotes from some reviews of the end
product of these meetings.

"An important work, because the author has dared to
explore the frontiers of professional responsibility.

"Dr. Dyce's concept of stress implies the discomfort of
realising the limitations of technical perfection for
making significant contributions to society. Based on
conclusions made following years of dialogue with a
variety of prominent and learned men and study at
Cambridge University, the author proposes the development of intellectual skills as crucial to making an impact
on the world...mankind is socially and politically short-
sighted, not by an inability to see, but by not taking the
time and effort to ask the right questions...stress is
viewed as a movement from the philosophy OF practice to
philosophy IN practice, i.e. 'asking the right questions' to

understand the world in which man lives. This book addresses a range of profound ideas that are not the ordinary province of the technically orientated professions...His ideas have implications for the importance of a liberal education for health professionals and a movement from the self-centered focus of the profession...some exceedingly interesting ideas and perceptions...concepts for thoughtful consideration." U.S.A.[1]

"Far reaching implications...Our problems within such a profession as dentistry are global in their extent and yet they lie, in the author's words, beyond our clinical experience, and so do the solutions. In our professional toil we strive to become more and more successful – but – what is success? For most of us, sadly, our goals of 'success' are measured in altogether the wrong 'units', and in our effort to amass these 'units', we conduct a dangerous and destructive contest with stress itself. Dr. Dyce suggests a new set of units, a new ethos, within which to conduct our professional lives: new and revolutionary, indeed, because it embodies direction and purpose.

"It is hard to disentangle the profession's development and role from the daily exigencies of practice, and this difficulty is addressed by the author in a way you may never come across elsewhere." U.K.[2]

"Investigates the catalyst of our ideas, and does not flinch from the analysis." France [3]

"Dyce was coaxed out of his shell into a world unknown to him, and challenged to explore the depths of society around him.

"Every doctor who considers himself successful should read this book. It will fill a void in his professional life, that he never knew existed." U.S.A.[4]

"Technical success is not enough – new thinking is required." Australia[5]

"Dyce sketches the 'immunology system' for decision-making. Stress is for Dyce a challenge towards proficiency and integrity... a spur to find out the right answers to the demands of life." Switzerland[6]

The book was called *Stress, the Dilemma of Success*, which emerged from thinking in the company of the academic life at the University of Cambridge. It was also my response to the early challenge of one of Frank Buchman's friends: "You doctors are dead, you don't contribute a damned thing to the thinking that needs to be done for the world. You do great work and you write about it, but you leave the thinking to others and you are equipped to do it."

We possess brains, trained in orderly thinking, which through generations have become obsessed with clinical expertise. These brains now need to be released to discover and articulate new truth. If we find universal truth at the heart of decision-making, then we have a new and valid offering to make to the affairs of men away beyond our care for the health of the body.

Is there a defence system (an immune system) for decision-making which filters off the wrong ideas?

What is an immune system for decision-making?

What is an immune system?

When we are sick and our physician gives us some pills, what do they do? They 'hold the line' while our own defence system (our immune system), creates the defence mechanism (antibody) which works and stops the sickness.

The proposition is that we have this inbuilt physical defence system. Personal matters, all day long, require constant choosing of answers to questions. Do we have a defence system to deal with this?

When we add Smith's Triangle (Initiative,Values,Impartial Spectator), we uncover this latent and already available defence system for all decision-making. The proposition then is: if we have difficulty in choosing which answer to a question, there is confusion in the mind. When this happens, the mind has a cross-current of signals and these, referred to the body, produce a cross-current of body chemistry. We then feel ill as a result and we call this stress.

When the choices of answers to the question are resolved, we have only one answer, not a mix, then the signals are clear, the body chemistry stops having cross-currents and we stop feeling ill.

This is of course destined to be called an oversimplification. But if you push the electric switch there is light, and I suppose that could also be called an oversimplification.

When we apply Smith's I.V.I.S. confusion is sorted out. No doubt, an oversimplification. But true.

Stress is NOT the confusion of choices of answers. That is strain or even breakdown.

Stress is the normal process of meeting/facing all questions, and learning to choose the single answer.

Stress is therefore the normal process of sorting out the myriad questions of everyday life.

This inbuilt faculty is available only when we are honest about our motives and learn about the application of the guidance of God. The man within the breast. Call it what you will.

The physical body carries a full range of defence particles (antibodies) which fit the intruders (antigens) as a key fits a lock, rendering the antigen inactive. The blood stream goes on to subdivide its defensive system into three parts. The first disposes of redundant parts of our structure. The second builds up memory of past intrusions of foreign invaders ready for any new assault. The third surveys potential hazards in future. We have the full development of similar reviewing in our decision-making process.

Until now immunology has been looked upon as a branch of medicine. But it is a discipline in its own right.

We are able to use its analytical capacity, all the ideas we call learning, and thus to sort out and clarify our decision-making.

The age of information technology will produce results which it would take the human brain 'for ever' to work out. We need to look beyond the myth of the infallibility of the artificial intelligence machine. Myth it is, because what we *DO* with the information is what will decide how the world goes.

Without more accurate wisdom (the defensive immune system) in decision-making, more information will not help us.

It is important to be analytical if we are to experience the central surprise. The surprise we face is that the same analytical process (as used in the defence of the body) is the key to the confusing self-will now raging through decision-making. The surprise is that the cell biologist teaches us these three lessons. Mentally we can do what the body does: leave the past behind; deal with the current intrusions into our correct decision-making; become alert to the future.

What decision to make? Which route to take? How can I be sure that my hopes will turn out to have been achieved? Do I have to go on keeping 25 balls in the air? Strain is a hazard for any successful professional or so it seems, unless we learn that there is a single right answer and we stop juggling with the opportunities of Name, Fame and Fortune. Stress is a fully recognised physiological force, that is, it is a normal bodily function. However difficult the situation, you can be at full throttle and at peace. The 25-hour day started for me at the age of 17.

Many offerings on the subject of stress make headlines in the popular press. They offer re-organisation of the office and staff or the hopeful understanding of managers etc. Few go to the structure of the body's well proven defence/immune system for guidance. There we accepted that in-built were defence particles (antibodies) which matched the invaders and cancelled their activity. Our own body was dealing with the invader.

The accompanying inflammation at the heart of decision-making needs to be examined, for if it is dealt with, by the in-built defence factor, Smith's triangle (Initiative/Values/Impartial spectator) can get on with dealing with the intruder. We will have made the right decision.

In general dental practice we may look into a mouth and quite readily come up with several different possible programmes for treatment. Each one can be supported. We say:

1. This plan would improve the patient's smile. 2. This one would be within the patient's budget. 3. This one ideal, but very expensive. 4. This one would fit nicely into the academic paper I am writing; I could do with more statistics. 5. This one is what the patient wants and is impossible.

But how do we choose? How do we decide?

Our *creative hopes* may be challenged by our personal planned financial requirements. Our *clinical judgement* may be challenged by the fact that this patient may not be ready for vast restoration of the mouth. Our *personal* operative skills may be challenged by our lack of instruction in advanced skills. Our early view that *pleasure is the target for life*, may be challenged by today's requirement of universal truth.

Much of the above can be dismissed as author's nonsense, because we can say that experience lays down exactly what decision to take. This will be true much of the time. However, every time we make a clinical decision we bump into our motives. By not labelling them, we become vulnerable to strain, put up with 'pressure', complain about it, go home exhausted, remain isolated from the formative thinking the world needs.

When my senior partner raised with me that every mouth was NOT a place for me to show off my skills, but belonged to the patient, he was beginning the process of my understanding that while three academic qualifications might have taught me to read a mouth, they had not taught me to read people.

It becomes clear that the core truth at the heart of decision-making is to recognise two factors: *Know How* and *Motives*. Confusion in the latter means confusion of signals in body chemistry and there has to be stress disorder, with the accompanying discomfort.

An undefended system for decision-making is vulnerable to four antigens: *Money: Ideology: Compromise: Ego* (MICE for short). And it is not difficult to think out the implications of each of these four, and the implications internationally as well as personally.

Why is it important to be as analytical about these as the cell biologist is in his search for the mechanisms of health? Because the world needs a new type of research worker. Men who will develop and articulate the structure for determining correct answers.

Why is this necessary?

On television I am deluged with the whims and fancies of media opinion. Someone speaks with the authority of his past experience, that the way ahead is his way. He is followed by someone else, equally supported by past experience, that his experience demands we proceed in the opposite direction. Each experience is valid, but my country is divided down the middle. Men who rely on past experience do not live with the real issues, however splendid their past experience. We must have a new dimension.

If the cell biologist has introduced us to the marvels of the body's defences and we have experience of personal change in our own motives with the resolution of conflict, why not discover the dimension of the grand design of the entire personality?

Stress then becomes the harnessing of our full potential. It is not a hazard at all. It is the acceptance of each day's challenge, and we learn to live one day at a time, assured that our defence system is on the alert.

Another of the secrets which is of great value is that when things are very difficult, we may feel that there is nothing we can do about the problems, we can return to our personal evidence from the past for re-assurance, and we can lay the problems down, with the confidence that resolution will occur as before.

The relationship between this very brief statement of today's possibilities and the vast uncertainty facing capitalism, suggests that resolution of tomorrow's problems is something new, which we are now obliged to look at.

The brief reports I have made of the thinking of Henry Drummond, Frank Buchman, and my own investigation of stress in professional life, reinforce my conviction that a very large challenge, away beyond our current skills, awaits our immediate attention. We develop the full dimension of Adam Smith's Triangle, and it is not a mystery. Our skill and *initiative* advances, our review of what is right for the people we look after develops our *values*, there is the unscrambling of motives by the *Impartial Spectator*.

Our I.V.I.S. is of equal importance to our D.N.A.

Chapter 10
A GLOBAL WRIT ON OFFER

The currently expressed vision for Europe is solidly related to the world economic market. As it is presented, it does not accept the grand design of Adam Smith. It takes no account of the dimension we have to deal with. Will Europe pick up the writ?

Unlimited individualistic laissez-faire economics is NOT the teaching of Adam Smith.

"The Scottish Enlightenment of the 18th century, had a special theoretical tool, which the French had not, to tackle the problem. That is political economy interwoven with moral philosophy. Is it possible for ordinary men to build the long bridge from the love of self to love of the universe.?"[1]

A writ is a command or precept or instrument, enjoining the person or persons to whom it is addressed to do some act specified therein. Today the requirement is a fresh study of the future of civilisation, no less: whether this civilisation will survive or fall.

Because of our excellence in our calling, we have the authority to proceed with the research facing all of us. It is not a party political social conflict. We are dealing with matters beyond the parish, the nation, the corporate agreements of groups of nations. Adam Smith's grand design will show that today's global advance in economics, beyond nation, beyond culture, has to be supported by two more factors. His research laid down some of the fundamental requirements.

While accepting our global skills in economics, inspired leadership is the need of the hour. The dimension awaiting our attention is at present being swallowed up by media coverage of revolution, all over the world. The word civilisation needs to be read as you and me and how we think and live, otherwise the acquisitors decide our fate. Ordinary men and women will eventually rise and object, but will it be soon enough?

When airports are solid with people going for holidays abroad and elsewhere millions are starving to death, the social change in the world again calls for an understanding of the word civilisation. When some eminent thinkers see in history a clearly defined pattern which declares that we are headed for a crash, and others see the pattern quite clearly as well, but indicate that this need not happen, then attention must be paid to their signals.

History, according to the first offering, follows a certain pattern which is observable and can be used to forecast the future course of events (historical determinism). It makes quite clear, however, that humanity can make its own destiny and there is no need for fatalism.

History, according to the second offering, illustrates that the brilliant thinking of individual leaders has until now been paternalistic toward their own nation and culture.

Both have a vast leap ahead of them on two scores. How do you think for civilisation, not nation or culture? How do you convince the voters who put you in power and whose first concerns are their own private lives? We need to shed our customary caution, built-in with scientific discipline and polite modesty.

Why should my life be decided by a global economic empire where I have no say in the matter? We have success in our professional skills in the care of people, and as presented in the national press many global economists are playing a game like a lottery. The more skilled managers are at producing a well run business, the more likely they are to attract the attention of others who appear to do little else but buy and sell portfolios.

We need to encourage those with the predisposition for research. It is reported that the man who invented the biology of the future (man's first explanation of how a gene works) knocked at many conventional doors in vain. "An indifferent French academic world was on course to miss completely a body of discoveries that was to constitute the greatest success story in biology of this century".[2] Francois Jacob's work "was a highly Socratic affair, concealing a secret attention to what other researchers could not see as yet." "Jacob: 'Contrary to what was long my belief, experimental science does not set out to explain the unknown in terms of the known, as in certain mathematical proof...but the opposite.'" "In other words, the truly new and promising fields of investigation are those whose existence no one suspects."

If the surface signs of the media are to be taken as those of today's architects of Europe, it is a mix of market trapeze acts being learned, with all the requirements of national self-defence, and a deep feeling of global change and a general lack of security. For the man who has a prime commitment to his trade, the juggling of bank rates, rise and fall of currencies, is summed up in the words of two very eminent French economists, Albert and Boissonnat in their book: *Stop Go Crash Boom*. "The real rules of the game are that international institutions are only permitted to tell the truth in economic matters if they do so in language that is so unintelligible to the general public that there is no risk of upsetting any government." "Censorship by text dilution."[3]

Typical of this outlook is Edward de Bono's book *Tactics*.[4] "I would not want to get into an argument as to whether people can or cannot change their personality." The core truth presented by de Bono is typical of our era of inventiveness and total failure to appreciate that our civilisation will rise or fall depending on whether our personality changes or not. One gets the impression that all 51 interviewees in the book, splendid people, have made millions, and what have we got? Against the needs of civilisation, we require a fresh approach to success.

Does the international debate on economics have to be likened to the biological research into the cause of cancer, with no single key mechanism of cause to be marked out? Not with Adam Smith.

Jean Monnet, whose efforts culminated in the establishment of the European Economic Community, attempted to hold together men of various countries after

World War II, to continue a supra-national attitude, but governments took individual control of their countries and pursued private political ends. Does this mean that we can only learn from our mistakes? Monnet and his international friends lost out to the governments of the day.

A wise observer of Smith and his contemporaries, Duncan Forbes, quotes one of them: "Human nature in fact is like a meteor, which shines only when it is in movement and as a result of friction. Man is happiest and best adjusted when all his powers are called forth and stretched to the utmost in and for his community... a nation flourishes in times of conflict, internal and external."

To pick up the global writ, Europe needs to move on from today's position of having a place in the world market place. The so often contrary and powerful waste of energy displayed in today's antinomies is a vast handicap, which will decide if this civilisation continues or falls.

If there is one lesson to be learned from a study of Adam Smith, it is the need for people who have true perspective. Freedom without perspective is today's illusion. All the faiths have to offer is the assurance that a dimension beyond the thinking of men, however brilliant it be, is normal and unfolding. The possibility of constructing a picture which allows every single person to have a unique personality, there for the discovery, is left out at our peril. In fact, freedom without this perspective is a drowning pool of ideas.

So, how can any organisation operate if everyone is special? Well, how is it that every D.N.A. is unique and we all live on the same planet, eat, sleep, breathe, go about our daily toil? That's the fascination of the project. Smith never gives the impression that to include the Impartial Spectator made a man religious looking or gave the impression that spiritual matters were for sometime after death.

Conclusions have to be drawn:

My contention is that we have two matters of great importance today. They are the deeper implications of two words: Antinomy and Civilisation.

The excellent, authoritative, so often contrary view of many who carry major decision-making, which affects the lives of millions, has now to be seen as not adequately related to the crisis in civilisation.

The fact that my 'foothills' of evidence may be different from yours, may not be used as a measure to be applied as we face the next higher hill. All we have proved is that there was a right answer for the 'hill' we last climbed. Today's multi-science has brought world cultures into bold relief. There is an answer to antinomy. And with it, the route to the next plateau for civilisation.

As with the chemical D.N.A. fingerprint, the I.V.I.S. fingerprint is as old as the hills and more. If it is complicated, we can take it that the presenter has not gone far enough himself. The question we must ask ourselves is: "Does my evidence shine?"

Are we just black holes?

We all stay on this planet and do not fly off into space because gravity keeps us in place. A brick thrown in the air returns to earth because of the force of gravity. A fun-rocket flies up and down it comes, by gravity's pull. This force is a major element in the mechanism of outer space.

Small stars have chemical/electrical commotions going on which produce light, travelling at 136,000 miles per second towards us. There are some hundred thousand million stars in our galaxy and a hundred thousand million galaxies.

The cosmologists' special interest today is in black holes out there in the sky at night. They say that a black hole was a star which was so large and its force of gravity so powerful that this had an immediate effect on the particles which fly about during chemical/electrical activity on its surface, before it exploded.

Light consists of fine particles and the cosmologist says that the light we see from other stars, we do not see from these very vast black hole stars, because the tremendous force of gravity of these stars pulls on the particles (of which the beam consists) and that beam of light never gets beyond the range of a fun rocket from the black hole star. So, we never see it, and the star explodes, leaving a black hole.

A good observation in the dimension of the universe,

and perhaps a useful measure of our meagre exploration of man's place in that universe.

Could we put the proposition: "Is my concern with myself so important (so intense) that I refer everything back to myself, with my 'force of gravity', such that my light never shines in the perspective of the universe? And no one really benefits." "Am I just another black hole star?" In terms of cosmology and the theory of relativity it is a possibility.

All the above has been spelled out, because today's initiative and values have a missing element which shouts at the heart of today's decision-making. How to deal with antinomy and civilisation.

Systasis: A word to describe the reconciliation of two valid and opposing ideas, a term used by Bacon (1605) and Sir Thomas Browne (1658). The new dimension required to move beyond antinomy, that blockage to the full development of initiative, which prevents us from reaching the next plateau. It is the central requirement in a world of revolution.

Civilisation: Today's global economic empires must be matched by similar vision in the fields of Values and the Impartial Spectator. This will happen when we deal with our antinomies.

The prospect is the rescue of Capitalism, through a vastly bigger idea. In fact the next dimension needed is a clear forward shift, and we may not call it capitalism any more.

The evidence is beyond speculation. To continue as we do now is just filling in time. That is not the attitude of responsible people.

Smith would have agreed with a great Englishman of the 20th century, Peter Howard, who said: "People need to be released from the prisons of their individual and collective histories."

Getting Adam Smith right is today's exercise in global thinking.

114

REFERENCES

T.M.S. The Theory of Moral Sentiments, Adam Smith.
R.B.L. Lectures on Rhetoric and Belles Lettres, Adam Smith.
C.A.S. Correspondence of Adam Smith, Adam Smith.
E.P.S. Essays on Philosophical Subjects, Adam Smith.

CHAPTER 1

Reference   1   T.V. jobs in the Press, Simon Clark, Director, The Media Monitoring Unit, The Times, 22 December 1989.
"Our research, reported in detail by The Times 15 August showed that, with regard to the daily quality press 68% of BBC Television's recruitment advertising over a six-month period was placed in The Guardian, compared with 16% in both The Independent and The Times, whilst 72% of the Independent Television's advertising was placed with the Guardian, 22% with The Independent and only 6% with The Times."

2   Time magazine. 14 April 1989 p53.

3   Stress, the Dilemma of Success, James Dyce, Stress Publications 1982.

4   An Essay on the History of Civil Society 1767, Adam Ferguson,
Edin.Univ.Press. 1966.(Forbes re Ferguson. Principles II)

5   Bantam 1989. P 127. P20. P30.

6   Collins Harvill 1988.

7   Bantam Press 1988.

8   A Story of Effective Statesmanship, Blandford 1956 and Grosvenor Books 1956 p42.

9   The Medusa and the Snail, Lewis Thomas. Penguin p43.

CHAPTER 2

Reference   1   The Rough New Game, Gerald Howard, The Author, Society of Authors, Autumn 1989 p18.

2   Adam Smith, The Man and His Works, E.G.West, Liberty Press. p43. Hutcheson.

3   ibidem p44

4   ibidem p47

5   ibidem p48

6   ibidem p54

7   R.B.L. i.6

8   Culture Shock, Gillian Upton, Managing your Business, Spring Issue. 1989

9   R.B.L. ii 126

10   Commemorative Symposium, Kirkcaldy 1973. Professor Hiroshi Mizuta, Meijo University, Nagoya.

11   R.B.L. ii. 129

12   E.P.S. I. 1

13   E.P.S. I. 6

14   E.P.S. II. 7

15   E.P.S. II. 12 (also W.N. V.i.f.25)

16   R.B.L. ii. 135-136
17   R.B.L. i. 1-5
18   R.B.L. i. 10
19   R.B.L. i. 62
20   R.B.L. i. v.66 – v.68
21   R.B.L. i. 70
22   R.B.L. ii. 18
23   R.B.L. i. 128
24   R.B.L. i. 168
25   R.B.L. i. 173
26   R.B.L. i. 190 – 191
27   R.B.L. ii. 16-17
28   R.B.L. ii. 55
29   R.B.L. ii. 59
30   R.B.L. ii. 252
31   Postscript, Adam Smith, The Man and His Works, E.G.West.Liberty.p232
32   Kirkcaldy Museum and Art Gallery. Andrea Kerr, Curator.
33   C.A.S. 207
34   C.A.S. 54
35   C.A.S. 54
36   C.A.S. 40
37   C.A.S. 40 addition

CHAPTER 3

Reference   1   The Trial of Socrates, I.F.Stone, Jonathan Cape. 1988 p158.
2   ibidem. from the Review by Lord Hailsham of St.Marylebone.
3   ibidem p115.
4   Acts of the Apostles, ch17 v15-34.
5   Confessions of St.Augustine. Two vols 7.20.
6   Apology of Socrates 21a.
7   T.M.S. VI. iii. 28
8   T.M.S. VI. iii. 28
9   T.M.S. I. iii. 1. 14 also Plato,Phaedo 1176 – e
10   Memorabilia by Xenophon 1.7 or 1-5
11   T.M.S, VII. ii. 2. 13
12   T.M.S. VI. iii. 5
13   Apology 30E
14   The Rt. Hon. Lord Hailsham of St. Marylebone.

CHAPTER 4

Reference   1   T.M.S. VI. ii. 2. 16 also VI.ii.2.17
2   T.M.S. II. iii. 1.4
3   T.M.S. III. 3.3
4   T.M.S. I. iii. 7
5   T.M.S. IV. 1. 6
6   T.M.S. III. 3. 4
7   T.M.S. VI concl 6th part
8   T.M.S. III. 3. 25
9   T.M.S. III. 2. 31
10   T.M.S. VI. 1. 12. also VI. 1. 11
11   T.M.S. III. 5.
12   T.M.S. III. 5. 7

13   T.M.S. I. iii. 2. 1
14   T.M.S. III. 3. 3
15   T.M.S. III. 2. 32

CHAPTER 5

Reference   1   C.A.S. letter 150, from David Hume on publication of
                  Wealth of Nations.
             2   The Founding Faith, John Kenneth Galbraith, Annals of
                  an abiding Liberal, Andre Deutch 1980.
             3   Former Provost. King's College, Cambridge.
             4   *Adam Smith and the Public Sector.* The Rt.Hon.John
                  Major M.P. (Adam Smith Institute, 27 June 1989.)
             5   *The Moral Case for the Free Market.* Rt.Hon.Nicholas
                  Ridley M.P. (Adam Smith Institute. 6 February 1990).
             6   Sir James Goldsmith. (Adam Smith Institute. 19 October
                  1989).
             7   How Democracies Perish, Jean-Francois Revel, Weiden-
                  feld and Nicolson 1955.
             8   Paris Notebook, J-F Revel. Encounter April 1988.
             9   Paris Notebook, J-F Revel. Encounter December 1985.
            10   Kingsway Publications. 1984 p142.
            11   The new left's assault on science, Beverly Halstead,
                  Salisbury Review. January 1987.
            12   Peter D. Howard.

CHAPTER 6

Reference   1   The Life of Henry Drummond, George Adam Smith,
                  Hodder & Stoughton 1899 p1.
             2   Natural Law in the Spiritual World, Henry Drummond
                  FRSE.FGS., Hodder & Stoughton 1885.p369.

CHAPTER 7

Reference   1   The Medusa and the Snail, Lewis Thomas, Penguin 1981.
             2   Dynamic out of Silence, Frank Buchman's relevance
                  today,
                  Theophil Spoerri, Grosvenor Books 1976.p125.
             3   ibidem p103.
             4   ibidem p206.
             5   ibidem p123.
             6   ibidem p104.
             7   ibidem p142.

CHAPTER 8

Reference   1   The Medusa and the Snail, Lewis Thomas, Penguin 1981.
             2   American Dental Society of London. 21 February 1962
             3   Remaking the World, Frank Buchman, Blandford 1961
             4   Moral Re-Armament News Letter 23. April 1989.
             5   Cogs in the Soviet Wheel, Mikhail Heller, Collins-Harvill
                  1989 p78 ref to V.I.Lenin. Sochineniya Vol45 p106.
             6   ibidem p56.
             7   The Dialectic of Change, Boris Kagarlitsky. Verso.
                  Review in Times 24 February 1990.

117

CHAPTER 9

Reference   1   Stress. The Dilemma of Success, J.M.Dyce, Stress Publications.
               Reviews in professional journals 1983
               Journal of Dental Education, U.S.A. John O. Odom.
            2   British Dental Journal, Kevin Lewis. January.
            3   Le Chirurgien Dentiste de France, May.
            4   American Academy of the History of Dentistry, Lloyd Church. October.
            5   Australian Dental Journal, June.
            6   SWISS Dent, 7-8.

CHAPTER 10

Reference   1   Professor Hiroshi Mizuta. Adam Smith Symposium. Kirkcaldy 6 June 1973.
            2   J-F Revel describing Francois Jacob's work.
            3   Stop Go Crash Boom, Albert & Boissonnat, Macdonald 1989.
            4   Tactics, Collins 1985.

SOME REQUIRED READING

The essays which this book comprises follow contemplation of some marking times in the professional life of the author, and the encouragement offered from the writing in the following books. Vast quantities of fresh ideas lie within. I look upon them as required reading. Other readers will find many jewels I have not recorded. Quotes have been recorded as accurately as possible. If any are missed may I make amends by recommending the researcher read the book.

The Theory of Moral Sentiments, Adam Smith, edited by Raphael & Macfie, Liberty Classics. ISBN 0-86597-012-2 (pbk)

Lectures on Rhetoric and Belles Lettres, Adam Smith, edited by Bryce, Liberty Classics. ISBN 0-86597-052-1 (pbk)

Correspondence of Adam Smith, edited by Mossner and Ross Liberty Classics. ISBN 0-913966-99-1 (pbk)

Essays on Philosophical Subjects., Adam Smith, edited by Wightman Bryce Liberty Classics. ISBN 0-86597-023-8 (pbk)

Adam Smith, the Man and his Works, E.G.West, Liberty Press. ISBN 0-913966-07-X (pbk)

Adam Smith (Past Masters), D.D.Raphael, Oxford Univ. Press. ISBN 0-19-287558-2 (pbk)

Adam Smith, Commemorative Symposium, Kirkcaldy 1973, Kirkcaldy District Council, KY1 1XW

Natural Law in the Spiritual World, Henry Drummond, Hodder and Stoughton. 1885

An Essay on the History of Civil Society, 1767, Adam Ferguson, edited, with an introduction by Duncan Forbes, Edinburgh University Press. 1966

Frank Buchman: A Life, Garth Lean, Constable, London. ISBN 0-09-466650-4

Peter Howard, Life and Letters, Anne Wolrige Gordon, Hodder and Stoughton. ISBN 340-10840-1

Dynamic out of Silence, Frank Buchman's relevance today, Theophil Spoerri, Grosvenor Books, London. ISBN 0-901269-19-0 (pbk)

The Medusa and the Snail, Lewis Thomas, Penguin Books. 1981 (pbk)

How Democracies Perish, Jean-Francois Revel, Weidenfeld and Nicolson. ISBN 0-297-78644-X

Cogs in the Soviet Wheel, Mikhail Heller, Collins Harvill. ISBN 0-00-272516-9

Perestroika, Mikhail Gorbachev, Collins. ISBN 0-00-215660-1

Thinkers of the New Left, Roger Scruton, Longman. ISBN 0-582-90273-8

A Brief History of Time, Stephen W. Hawking, Bantam Press. ISBN 0-593-01518-5

The Trial of Socrates, I.F.Stone, Jonathan Cape. ISBN 0-224-02591-0

The Great Depression of 1990, Dr. Ravi Batra, Bantam Books. ISBN 0-553-17629-3

STOP GO CRASH BOOM, Michael Albert and Jean Boissonat, Macdonald Books. ISBN 0-356-18657-1

About the Author

James Dyce's six previous books, technical, clinical, and also about fishing, reflect experience of many years of practice in Harley Street. He graduated in Medicine in Scotland and took a further doctorate in Dentistry in America. He has lectured to his profession in America, Australia, Japan, South Africa and Europe. He set up a new department at Guy's Hospital.

Anyone who lives the twentyfive hour day, is familiar with Stress. Dyce's recent books on stress have earned these review notices:

"Should be read by everyone . . . Not to do so would be to leave a void which others may be unable to fill."

"The Scots have a knack of pioneering . . . James Watt, Adam Smith, Livingstone . . . James Dyce is in that tradition in his books on Stress."

The author decided that world instability calls for time to search beyond the skills and wisdoms of today.

Dyce worked at the University of Cambridge as a research scholar for three and a half years. He decided that the specialist of today needs the grand design of thinkers like Adam Smith.